TABLE OF INDEX

MW00951137

TABLE OF INDEX

INSTRUCTIONS

The answers to each problem is in the back of this book, section 100.0.   I think it is best for the parents to remove this part of the book.

Calculators are allowed only on question that start with the number 4, or the Geometry section

 The problems might not be in sequential order.   Don't worry its correct.

If you don't get the correct answer, and want an explanation on how to work the problem, go to youtube and type in "MMT" then the problem number. An example would be "MMT 3.9.w12" The video will show you how to work problem 3.9.w12.

For one on one tutoring via skype at $35.00/Hr.; contact me at marksmathtutoring@yahoo.com

REFERENCES

LENGTH

ENGLISH

1 mile (mi) = 1,760 yards (yds)
1 yard (yd) = 3 feet (ft)
1 foot (ft) = 12 inches (in)

METRIC

1 kilometer (km) = 1,000 meters (m)
1 meter (m) = 100 centimeters (cm)
1 centimeters (cm) = 10 millimeters (mm)

VOLUME AND CAPACITY

ENGLISH

1 gallon (gal) = 4 quarts (gt)
1 quart (qt) = 2 pints (pt)
1 pint (pt) = 2 cups (c)
1 cup © = 8 fluid ounces (fl oz)

METRIC

1 liter = 1,000 millimeters (ml)

WEIGHT AND MASS

ENGLISH

1 ton (T) = 2,000 pounds (lb)
1 pound (lb) = 16 ounces (oz)

METRIC

1 kilogram (kg) = 1,000 grams (g)
1 gram (g) = 1,000 milligrams (mg)

TIME

1 year = 12 months
1 year = 52 weeks
1 week = 7 days
1 day = 24 hours
1 hour = 60 minutes
1 minute = 60 seconds

REFERENCES

PERIMETER

Square	4 X SIDE = PERIMETER
Rectangle	LENGTH + LENGTH + SIDE + SIDE = PERIMETER

AREA

Square	SIDE X SIDE = AREA
Rectangle	LENGTH X SIDE = AREA

 Croquis of a Deliberate Crime

YouTube

If you don't get the correct answer, and want an explanation on how to work the problem, go to youtube and type in "MMT" then the problem number. An example would be, MMT 3.9.w12,. The video will show you how to work problem 3.9.w12.

For one on one tutoring via skype at $35.00/Hr.; contact me at marksmathtutoring@yahoo.com

DEFINITIONS

Sum is the answer after adding the numbers

Product is the answer after dividing the numbers

Difference is the answer after subtracting the numbers

Congruent means if two shapes have the same shape and size of each other. They don't need two have the same orientation. In other words one can be up side down from the other.

Lines of symmetry is a line that divides a shape into two equal size and shape. Two examples are shown below

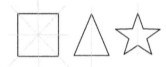

Vertical Line of Symmetry the shape can be divided into two equal sizes and shapes about a vertical line

Horizontal Line of Symmetry the shape can be divided into two equal sizes and shapes about a horizontal line

Transition The object remains the same size and shape but is slide or moved up down or to the side

Rotational Transition The object remains the same size and shape but is rotated or spun around

Reflection Transition The object remains the same size and shape but is flipped over and would have the image a mirror would give

Right Angle: The measure of the angle is 90 degrees

Serza is a 7 sided figure. It is also called a heptagon. Example is below.

Rhombus is a figure with four side all of equal length. All Rhombuses are parallelograms and kites. A square is a Rhombus with all 90 degree angle. A diamond, or kite shape is also a Rhombus. Two example are below.

Square is a parallelogram with 4 right angle (90 degrees), or a Quadrilaterals with 4 right angles with four sides of equal length

Kite: Is a Rhombus with angles that are not right angles (90 degrees)

Parallelogram has two sets of parallel lines. The opposite sides are of equal length.

Trapezoid four sided figure with one set of parallel sides.

Rectangle is a parallelogram with 4 right angle (90 degrees), or said another way a Quadrilaterals with 4 right angles

Polygons is a figure that would lie flat on a table. It is made up of straight lines and is closed, or could be used to contain your dog like a fence. Any shape will do as long as it is flat and closed, or no open gates in the fence.

Quadrilaterals Is a polygon with four side and four edges. The following are some examples

Pentagons is a five sided polygon

Hexagons is a six sided polygon. Example is below

Vertices means corner.

Edge is a line where two planes or sheet meet. Where the wall joins to the flour is a edge.

Parallel lines: two lines that never change the distance between them

Acute Angle: angle less than 90 degrees

Obtuse Angle: angle greater than 90 degrees

Right Angle: angle equal to 90 degrees

NUMBERS

Even is a whole number that is divisible by two. The best way at your age to determine this is start with 2 and count up by 2s. Ex 2, 4, 6, 8, 10, etc. If you say the number it is even.

Odd whole number that is not even. The last digit of the number is a 1,3,5,7,or a 9. Examples of add number would ne 221, 683, 66889, or 7.

ONES PLACE: is the place holding the smallest value. The underlined bold number is in the ones place in these examples: 2**4**, 34**6**, 48**6**, 126**7**, 32**5**, 67**9**,1125**8**

TENS PLACE: IS the smallest value that can divided by 10 evenly. The underlined bold number is in the tens place in these examples: 2**3**6, **4**5, 57**7**8, 825**7**8, **5**4, 1**2**8, 7**7**8

HUNDREDS PLACE: TENS PLACE: IS the smallest value that can divided by 100 evenly. The underlined bold number is in the hundreds place in these examples: **1**27, 3**4**67, 5**7**88, 3**2**75, **3**46

THOUSANDS PLACE: IS the smallest value that can divided by 1000 evenly. The underlined bold number is in the THOUSANDS place in these examples: **3**276, 4**5**887, **2**457, 11**2**78, 12**8**95

Interest Is the extra money you pay back. If you borrow $200 and pay back $210, the interest is $10.

UNITS

Units of weight: pounds, grams, ounces, tones

Units of volume: Gallons, quarts, pints

Units of Length: Centimeter (cm), Millimeter (mm), Meter (m), Kilometer, Inch (in), Foot (ft), Mile

SYMBOLS

GREATER THAN: Uses the symbol > It mean the item on the left is greater than the item on the right. An example would be 8>3. In words this is eight is greater than 3. Remember the bird always eats the bigger worm.

LESS THAN: Uses the symbol < It mean the item on the left is less than the item on the right. An example would be 8<3. In words this is eight is greater than 3. Remember the bird always eats the bigger worm.

GREATER THAN OR EQUAL TO: Uses the symbol ≥ It mean the item on the left is greater than or equal to the item on the right. An example would be 8≥8. In words this is eight is greater than or equal to 8. Remember the bird always eats the bigger worm.

LESS THAN OR EQUAL TO: Uses the symbol ≤ It mean the item on the left is less than or equal to the item on the right. An example would be 8≤8. In words this is eight is greater than or equal to 8. Remember the bird always eats the bigger worm.

Mean: average means the same. Add all the number up and then divide by the total number of numbers you added

Median: Put the number is order of least to greatest. The number is the middle is the median. If there is two numbers in the middle then add them together and divide the sum by 2

Mode: The number that occurs most frequently in the data.

Croquis of a
Deliberate
Crime
YouTube

If you don't get the correct answer, and want an explanation on how to work the problem, go to YouTube and type in "MMT" then the problem number. An example would be, MMT 3.9.w12,. The video will show you how to work problem 3.9.w12.

For one on one tutoring via skype at $35.00/Hr.; contact me at marksmathtutoring@yahoo.com

2.0 LOGIC

2.1) What would be the best unit of measurement for the size of your dog?
a) Gallons, b) pounds, c) pints, d) Quart

2.2) You parents borrowed $5,000.00 from the bank to buy a car. They repaid $6,500.00. Which statement best explains why they paid the extra $1,500.00
a) They wanted to donate $1,500.00 to the bank to be nice
b) They repaid the loan on a week day and the bank charges money for these days
c) They had extra money and nothing to do with it.
d) The bank charged $1,500.00 in interest for a $6,000.00 loan

2.3) I'm thinking of a number. It has a 3 in the thousands place and a 4 in the hundreds place Which of the following could be the number I am think about?
a) 1,356
b) 3,247
c) 3,456
d) 4,389

2.4) I'm thinking of a number. It has a 4 in the thousands place and a 5 in the tens place. Which of the following could be the number I am think about?
a) 2,557
b) 1376
c) 4,157
d) 6578

2.5) I'm thinking of a number. It has a 2 in the tens place and a 7 in the ones place. Which of the following could be the number I am thinking about?
a) 137
b) 27
c) 331
d) 72

2.6) I'm thinking of a number. It has a 6 in the thousands place and a 8 in the ones place. Which of the following could be the number I am thinking about?
a) 8,236
b) 4,468
c) 4,648
d) 6,458

2.7) What number is in the hundreds palace of 137

2.8) What number is in the thousands place of 7,689

2.9) Which of the following has the same value of 6,315,256
a)6,000,000+300,000+5,000,+200+50+6
b)6,000,000+300,000+10,000+200+50+6
c)6,000,000+300,000+10,000+5,000,+200
d)6,000,000+300,000+10,000+5,000,+200+50+6

For one on one tutoring via skype at $35.00/Hr.; contact me at marksmathtutoring@yahoo.com

2.10) Which of the following has the same value of 140,312
a)100,000+140,000+3000+10+2
b) 1,400,000+40,000+300+10+2
c) 100,000+40,000+10+2
d) 100,000+40,000+300+10+2

2.11) The number 65.03 can be expressed as
a) (6X10)+(5X1)+(3X0.10)
b) (6X10)+(50X1)+(3X0.01)
c) (6X10)+(50X1)+(3X0.10)
d) (6X10)+(5X1)+(3X0.01)

2.12) The number 142.18 can be expressed as
a) (1X100)+(40X10)+(2X1)+(1X0.1)X(8X0.01)
b) (1X100)+(4X10)+(2X1)+(1X0.01)X(8X0.01)
c) (1X100)+(4X10)+(2X1)+(1X0.1)X(8X0.001)
d) (1X100)+(4X10)+(2X1)+(1X0.1)X(8X0.01)

2.13) What is the relationship between the hundreds place and the tens place in the number 4,221
a) The hundreds place is 2 times larger than the tens place
b) The hundreds place is 1 more than the tens place
c) The hundreds place is 10 times the tens place
d) There is no relationship between them.

2.14) What is the relationship between the thousands place and the hundreds place in the number 4,411
a) The hundreds place is 2 times larger than the tens place
b) The hundreds place is 1 more than the tens place
c) The thousands place is 10 times the hundreds place
d) There is no relationship between them.

2.15) Which statement about the number 48 is true
a) It is odd, because it can be divided by 3
b) It is even, because it can be divided by 2
c) It is even because 8+4=12 is even
d) It is even because 4 and 8 are both even

2.16) Which of the following numbers is even
a) 27, b) 32, c) 81, d) 127

2.17) Which of the following numbers is even
a) 236, b) 137, c) 5179, d) 331

2.18) Which of the following numbers is odd
a) 24, b) 377, c) 6428, d) 46

2.19) Which of the following numbers is odd
a) 45, b) 224, c) 56, d) 2246

2.20) Which of the following numbers is even
a) 2278, b) 321, c) 56797, d) 33

2.21) Which of the following numbers is odd
a) 3357, b) 324, a) 32, d) 124

4.22) Loren has six football jerseys hanging on the wall. Which ones are even numbered?

2.23) There are four glass of milk in the refrigerator. Glass A is 4 days older than glass B. Glass B is 6 days older than glass C. Glass C is twice the age as glass D. D is 3 days old. What is the combined age in days of all four glasses?

2.24) If you roll a dice and spin the spinner. How many combination with an odd number can occur?

2.25) Given the combinations of types of music at a party and snakes how many combination are possible?

MUSIC   SNACKS

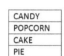

ROCK	
JAZZ	CANDY
CLASSICAL	POPCORN
POP	CAKE
OPERA	PIE

2.26) Given the options of clothing how many possible options are available?

SHIRTS   PANTS   SHOES

WHITE		
BLUE		
RED		SNEAKERS
GREEN	SHORTS	PUMPS
YELLOW	JEANS	BOOTS
	SLACKS	SANDELS

2.27) I am thinking of a number. There are three clues below.

 # The value of the digit 7 is (7X100)
 # The value of the digit 6 is (6X10)
 # The value of the digit 3 is (3X1)

Which of the following number could be the number I am thinking about

a) 367
b) 673
c) 763
d) 736

For one on one tutoring via skype at $35.00/Hr.; contact me at marksmathtutoring@yahoo.com

2.28) I am thinking of a number. There are three clues below.
   # The value of the digit 5 is (5X1000)
   # The value of the digit 5 is (5X10)
   # The value of the digit 4 is (4X1)
Which of the following number could be the number I am thinking about
a) 5054
b) 5145
c) 4154
d) 5545

2.29) A book has the weight of 3 kilograms. Which of the following could have the same mass.
a) a car
b) airplane
c) peanut
d) small cat

2.30) There four times as many birds as dogs in my neighborhood. There are three times as many cats as dogs. Which combination below could be the population of this neighborhood.

A) 12 dogs, 4 cats, 24 birds
B) 12 dogs, 4 cats, 3 birds
C) 12 dogs, 48 birds, 36 cats
D) 12 dogs, 4 cats, 4 cats

2.31) If I make cookies with the following rations
   # 64 chocolate
   # 23 mores oatmeal than chocolate
   # 17 more peanut butter than oatmeal
What is the total number of cookies I made

2.32) I caught 124.6 pounds of fish. My friend caught 3 times this. What was the weight of the fish he caught.

2.33) On my fishing trip I caught the following fish.
   # 236 mediums
   # 29 less then mediums were large
   # 69 more than mediums were small
How many small fish did I catch

2.34) What is the relationship between the number pairs below
 (12, 168), (8,112), (16,224), (18,252)
A) The first number is the quotient of the second divided by 14
B) The first number is the sum of the second plus 146
C) The first number is the product of the first multiplied by 8
D) The first number is the result of the first minus 146

Croquis of a
Deliberate
Crime
YouTube

3 ARITHMETIC

3.1 Addition-Single Digits

3.1.1) 1+3=   3.1.2) 2+0=   3.1.3) 4+6=   3.1.4) 5+8=   3.1.5) 3+2=   3.1.6) 7+3=
3.1.7) 3+0=   3.1.8) 7+9=   3.1.9) 1+8=   3.1.10) 5+5=   3.1.11) 7+4=   3.1.12) 2+6=
3.1.13) 4+5=   3.1.14) 5+9=   3.1.15) 2+5=   3.1.16) 6+9=   3.1.17) 4+2=   3.1.18) 3+8=
3.1.19) 2+2=   3.1.20) 4+8=   3.1.21) 8+2=   3.1.22) 9+5=   3.1.23) 6+4=   3.1.24) 8+5=
3.1.25) 4+7=   3.1.26) 8+7=   3.1.27) 9+9=   3.1.28) 9+0=   3.1.29) 6+6=   3.1.30) 2+7=
3.1.31) 1+2=   3.1.32) 7+8=   3.1.33) 6+2=   3.1.34) 3+4=   3.1.35) 9+4=   3.1.36) 1+5=
3.1.37) 7+6=   3.1.38) 8+8=   3.1.39) 9+6=   3.1.40) 1+6=   3.1.41) 6+5=   3.1.42) 9+2=

3.1.43)   7   3.1.44)   9   3.1.45)   3   3.1.46)   5   3.1.47)   8   3.1.48)   5
          +3   +4   +6   +9   +5   +7

3.1.49)   8   3.1.50)   7   3.1.51)   6   3.1.52)   7   3.1.53)   3   3.1.54)   2
          +8   +2   +4   +7   +2   +9

3.2 Addition-Two Digits

3.2.1)11+23=   3.2.2)22+20=   3.2.3)34+16=   3.2.4)65+68=   3.2.5)83+22=   3.2.6)33+60=
3.2.7)17+39=   3.2.8)81+48=   3.2.9)65+05=   3.2.10)37+74=   3.2.11)34+25=   3.2.12)85+39=
3.2.13)72+35=   3.2.14)16+49=   3.2.15)44+92=   3.2.16)92+12=   3.2.17)44+28=   3.2.18)28+32=
3.2.19)19+55=   3.2.20)36+54=   3.2.21)84+67=   3.2.22)98+27=   3.2.23)29+59=   3.2.24)19+40=
3.2.25)36+66=   3.2.26)11+62=   3.2.27)47+38=   3.2.28)76+12=   3.2.29)23+64=   3.2.30)79+54=
3.2.31)37+46=   3.2.32)18+88=   3.2.33)79+26=   3.2.34)31+56=   3.2.35)26+85=   3.2.36) 40+31=

3.2.37)   21   3.2.38)   57   3.2.39)   89   3.2.40)   65   3.2.41)   81   3.2.42)   51
          +34   +56   +32   +67   +83   +17

3.2.43)   75   3.2.44)   67   3.2.45)   32   3.2.46)   99   3.2.47)   27   3.2.48)   31
          +46   +76   +88   +37   +28   +98

3.3 Multiple Digit Addition

3.3.1)111+2365=   3.3.2)2227+201=   3.3.3)343+160   3.3.4)165+6825=
3.3.5)8301+22=   3.3.6)331+602=   3.3.7)1775+39=   3.3.8)811+483=
3.3.9)6523+105=   3.3.10)376+742=   3.3.11)345+255=   3.3.12)854+399=
3.3.13)726+355=   3.3.14)116+949=   3.3.15)44+192=   3.3.16)920+128=
3.3.17)445+287=   3.3.18)284+132=   3.3.19)119+855=   3.3.20)336+254=
3.3.21)284+367=   3.3.22)298+727=   3.3.23)29+2259=   3.3.24)119+409=
3.3.25)365+166=   3.3.26)110+627=   3.3.27)475+386=   3.3.28)768+129=
3.3.29)236+642=   3.3.30)790+543=   3.3.31)375+461=   3.3.32)182+888=
3.3.33)793+265=   3.3.34)314+5611=   3.3.35)2664+8551=   3.3.36)21+568=

3.3.37)   571   3.3.38)   2889   3.3.39)   1653   3.3.40)   781   3.3.41)   3256
          +343   +566   +327   +679   +124

3.3.42)   245   3.3.43)   175   3.3.44)   267   3.3.45)   132   3.3.46)   199
          +31   +46   +376   +988   +337

Decimal addition

3.12.1)11+2.3=
3.12.4)6.5+6.8=
3.12.7)1.7+3.9=
3.12.10)3.7+74=
3.12.13).72+35=
3.12.16)9.2+12=
3.12.19)11.1+2.365=
3.12.22)16.5+68.25=
3.12.25)1.775+3.9=
3.12.28)37.6+.742=

3.12.2).22+2.0=
3.12.5).83+2.2=
3.12.8)8.1+.48=
3.12.11)3.4+2.5=
3.12.14)1.6+4.9=
3.12.17)4.4+.28=
3.12.20)2.227+2.01=
3.12.23)83.01+2.2=
3.12.26)81.1+4.83=
3.12.29)34.5+25.5=

3.12.3)3.4+16=
3.12.6)3.3+60=
3.12.9).65+0.5=
3.12.12).85+39=
3.12.15).44+9.2=
3.12.18)2.8+3.2=
3.12.21)34.3+16.0
3.12.24)3.31+60.2=
3.12.27)65.23+10.5=
3.12.30).854+.399=

The table below shows the number of dogs with each color in a small town.

Color of dogs	Number of dogs
Black	215
white	167
yellow	132
brown	367
spotted	197

3.3.w1) How many dogs live in this small town?
3.3.w2) What is the total number of black, white and brown dogs living in this small town?
3.3.w3) How many spotted dogs live in this small town?
3.3.w4) What is the total number of brown and yellow dogs living in this small town?

The following table lists the number of lakes in each state

State	Number of Lakes
Illinois	23
Washington	71
California	82
Arizona	17
Kentucky	45
New York	67

3.3.w5) How many lakes are there in California?
3.3.w6) How many lakes are there in Arizona?
3.3.w7) What is the total number of lakes in Arizona Kentucky and New York?
3.3.w8) What is the total number of lakes listed in this table?

The following lists the number of vegetables Mary grew in her garden this year
    # onions 346
    #carrots 157
    #tomatoes 281
3.3.w9) How many carrots did Mary grow?
3.3.w10) What is the total number of vegetables Mary grew?
3.3.w11)What is the total number of onions and tomatoes that Mary grew?

For one on one tutoring via skype at $35.00/Hr.; contact me at marksmathtutoring@yahoo.com

The following is a series of numbers
      6, 10, 14, 18
3.3.w12) What would be the next two numbers in this series

3.3.w13) What number would not be in this series?
      a) 30, b) 38, c) 44, d) 50

3.3.w14) Which number represents the number 674
      a) 200+400+65+9
      b) 60+7+4
      c) 342+472
      d) 60+70+40
3.3.w15) You open a bank account with $127. The next week you deposit $312, followed by another $251 the next week. What is the amount in your bank account?

3.3.w16) I bought 1 cake for $12.83 and two pies for $15.61 each. What was the total cost of this purchase?

3.3.w17) The following table details the number of apples the school sold last week. What is the best estimate of the total number of apples sold last week?

DAY	NUMBER
Monday	132
Tuesday	247
Wednesday	331
Thursday	287
Friday	198

3.3.w18) The clock below shows the time I started to study.

If I study for 1 hour and 20 minutes which of the following digital clocks below shows the time of day I finished.
a)   c)

b)   d)

 Croquis of a
Deliberate
Crime
YouTube

For one on one tutoring via skype at $35.00/Hr.; contact me at marksmathtutoring@yahoo.com

3.3.w19) The clock below shown the time I started playing fetch with my dog.

If I played for 30 minutes which digital clock below shows the time I was finished?

a) **12:35**   c) **12:25**

b) **1:35**   d) **1:25**

3.3.w20) The following clock shows what time I started eating

If it takes me 45 minutes to eat which clock below shows the time I am finished

a)   d)

b)   c)

Croquis of a Deliberate Crime

YouTube

If you don't get the correct answer, and want an explanation on how to work the problem, go to YouTube and type in "MMT" then the problem number. An example would be, MMT 3.9.w12,. The video will show you how to work problem 3.9.w12.

For one on one tutoring via skype at $35.00/Hr.; contact me at marksmathtutoring@yahoo.com

3.3.w21) The clock below shows the time I started watching my favorite tv show.

If I watch for 25 minutes, which clock below shows the time I am finished.

a)   c)

b)   d)

3.3.w22) If the rule is add 48 to a number to get the answer which table below shows this relationship?

A)   B)

NUMBER	EXPRESSION	ANSWER
48	48+1	49
48	48+2	50
48	48+3	51
48	48-4	52

NUMBER	EXPRESSION	ANSWER
48	48x1	48
48	48-1	48
48	48+0	48
48	48-0	48

C)   d)

NUMBER	EXPRESSION	ANSWER
1	1+48	49
2	2+48	50
3	3+48	51
4	4+48	52

NUMBER	EXPRESSION	ANSWER
1	35+1	36
2	36+2	38
3	37+3	40
4	38+4	42

3.3.w23) A bakery makes 500 chocolate cupcakes per day . They make 135 more vanilla cupcakes per day than chocolate. Which equation below could be used to find X the total number of vanilla cupcakes per day.
a) x=500-135
b)x= 500+500+135
c) x= 500X135
d) x=500÷135

Croquis of a
Deliberate
Crime

YouTube

3.3.w24) The table below shows the number of apples compared with the number of oranges

APPLES	ORANGES
82	114
95	127
64	96
47	79
78	110

Which statement below describes the relationship in the table

a) The number of apples + 32 = number of oranges
b) The number of apples - 32 = number of oranges
c) The number of apples + 23 = number of oranges
a) The number of apples - 23 = number of oranges

3.3.w25)You can earn an extra points on a test if you do a special project. Which table below best represents your final score for the relationship Y = 35 + X

A)

INITAIL TEST SCORE	FINAL TEST SCORE
35	70
45	75
55	90
63	100

B)

INITAIL TEST SCORE	FINAL TEST SCORE
35	70
45	80
55	90
63	100

C)

INITAIL TEST SCORE	FINAL TEST SCORE
35	70
45	80
55	95
63	100

D)

INITIAL TEST SCORE	FINAL TEST SCORE
35	70
45	80
55	90
63	98

3.3.W26) The table below shows the number of fish I caught on vacation. If the total number is 127 which equation below would be the best way to determine the number I caught on the 4th day.

INITAIL TEST SCORE	FINAL TEST SCORE
1	32
2	17
3	42
4	n

A) 127= (32+17+42)-N
B) 127=(32+17+42)+N
C) 127=(32+17+42)xN
D) 127=(32+17+42)÷N

Croquis of a Deliberate Crime

YouTube

3.3.w27) The relationship between y and x is defined by Y = 2.05 + X. Which table below best represents this relationship.

A)

X	Y
17.3	19.35
18.5	20.55
25.1	27.25
31.8	33.85

B)

X	Y
17.3	19.35
18.5	20.75
25.1	27.15
31.8	33.85

C)

X	Y
17.3	19.15
18.5	20.55
25.1	27.15
31.8	33.85

D)

X	Y
17.3	19.35
18.5	20.55
25.1	27.15
31.8	33.85

3.3.W28) Two sequences of number are listed in the table below.

Sequence A	7.8	12.3	14.7	16.4
Sequence B	13.1	17.6	20.0	21.7

Which statement below best represents this relationship
A) Sequence A is 5.3 less than Sequence B
B) Sequence B is 4.5 less than Sequence A
C) Sequence A is 5.3 more than Sequence B
D) Sequence B is 5.3 less than Sequence A

3.3.w29) If I start my homework at 2:45 and work for 1 hour and 45 minutes what time do I finish

3.3.w30) If I start to read at 5:20 and do it for 2 hours and 50 minutes what time do I finish

3.3.w31) If I start to do something at 1:30 and continue for 2hours and 30 minutes what time do I finish

3.3.w32) If I start to play with my dog at 3:15 and do so for 2 hours and 15 minutes what time do I finish

3.4 Subtraction-Single Digits

3.4.1) 5-3=	3.4.2) 2-0=	3.4.3) 8-6=	3.4.4) 9-8=	3.4.5) 3-2=	3.4.6) 7-3=
3.4.7) 3-0=	3.4.8) 7-4=	3.4.9) 1-1=	3.4.10) 5-4=	3.4.11) 7-4=	3.4.12) 2-1=

3.4.55) 1-3=	3.4.56) 2-10=	3.4.57) 4-6=	3.4.58) 9-8=	3.4.59) 13-2=	3.4.60) 7-6=
3.4.61) 3-0=	3.4.62) 7-9=	3.4.63) 1-8=	3.4.64) 5-5=	3.4.65) 7-4=	3.4.66) 2-6=
3.4.67) 4-5=	3.4.68) 5-9=	3.4.69) 2-5=	3.4.70) 6-9=	3.4.71) 4-2=	3.4.72) 3-8=
3.4.73) 2-2=	3.4.74) 4-8=	3.4.75) 8-2=	3.4.76) 9-5=	3.4.77) 6-4=	3.4.78) 8-5=
3.4.79) 4-7=	3.4.80) 8-7=	3.4.81) 9-9=	3.4.82) 9-0=	3.4.83) 6-6=	3.4.84) 2-7=
3.4.85) 1-2=	3.4.86) 7-8=	3.4.87) 6-2=	3.4.88) 3-4=	3.4.89) 9-4=	3.4.90) 1-5=
3.4.91) 7-6=	3.4.92) 8-8=	3.4.93) 9-6=	3.4.94) 1-6=	3.4.95) 6-5=	3.4.96) 9-2=

3.4.97) 7 -9	3.4.98) 9 -4	3.4.99) 3 -6	3.4.100) 5 -9	3.4.101) 8 -5	3.4.102) 5 -7

3.4.103) 8 -8	3.4.104) 7 -2	3.4.105) 6 -4	3.4.106) 7 -7	3.4.107) 3 -2	3.4.108) 2 -9

3.5 Subtraction-Two Digits

3.5.1)81-23=   3.5.2)22-20=   3.5.3)34-16=   3.5.4)65-28=   3.5.5)83-22=   3.5.6)33-20=

3.5.7)97-39=   3.5.8)81-48=   3.5.9)65-05=   3.5.10)87-74=   3.5.11)34-25=   3.5.12)85-39=

3.5.13)72-5=   3.5.14)56-49=   3.5.15)44-12=   3.5.16)92-2=   3.5.17)44-28=   3.5.18)88-32=

3.5.19)19-15=   3.5.20)86-54=   3.5.21)84-67=   3.5.22)98-27=   3.5.23)59-29=   3.5.24)79-40=

3.5.25)36-6=   3.5.26)61-10=   3.5.27)47-38=   3.5.28)76-2=   3.5.29)23-4=   3.5.30)79-54=

3.5.31)37-16=   3.5.32)18-9=   3.5.33)79-26=   3.5.34)31-6=   3.5.35)86-85=   3.5.36) 17-8

3.5.37) 81	3.5.38) 57	3.5.39) 89	3.5.40) 65	3.5.41) 81	3.5.42) 45
-34	- 6	-32	-47	-73	-1

3.5.43) 75	3.5.44) 67	3.5.45) 32	3.5.46) 99	3.5.47) 27	3.5.48) 67
-46	- 6	-18	-37	-18	-38

3.5.49)11-23=   3.5.50)22-30=   3.5.51)34-16=   3.5.52)65-48=   3.5.53)13-22=   3.5.54)33-60=

3.5.55)17-39=   3.5.56)81-48=   3.5.57)65-95=   3.5.58)37-74=   3.5.59)34-85=   3.5.60)85-39=

3.5.61)72-35=   3.5.62)16-49=   3.5.63)44-92=   3.5.64)92-12=   3.5.65)44-28=   3.5.66)28-32=

3.5.67)19-55=   3.5.68)36-54=   3.5.69)84-67=   3.5.70)98-27=   3.5.71)29-59=   3.5.72)19-40=

3.5.73)36-66=   3.5.74)11-62=   3.5.75)47-38=   3.5.76)76-12=   3.5.77)23-64=   3.5.78)79-54=

3.5.79)37-46=   3.5.80)18-88=   3.5.81)79-26=   3.5.82)31-56=   3.5.83)26-85=   3.5.84) 40-31=

3.5.85) 21	3.5.86) 57	3.5.87) 89	3.5.88) 65	3.5.89) 81	3.5.90) 51
-34	-56	-32	-67	-83	-17

3.5.91) 75	3.5.92) 67	3.5.93) 32	3.5.94) 99	3.5.95) 27	3.5.96) 31
-46	-76	-88	-37	-28	-98

3.6 Subtraction-Multiple digit

3.6.1)1111-365=   3.6.2)2227-201=   3.6.3)343-160   3.6.4)165-25=   3.6.5)8301-22=

3.6.6)1331-302=   3.6.7)1775-39=   3.6.8)811-483=   3.6.9)6523-105=   3.6.10)976-742=

3.6.11)345-255=   3.6.12)854-99=   3.6.13)726-355=   3.6.14)116-49=   3.6.15)244-192=

3.6.16)920-128=   3.6.17)445-287=   3.6.18)284-12=   3.6.19)1119-855=   3.6.20)336-254=

3.6.21)284-167=   3.6.22)798-727=   3.6.23)1129-159=   3.6.24)119-9=   3.6.25)365-166=

3.6.26)1110-627=   3.6.27)475-386=   3.6.28)768-129=   3.6.29)236-42=   3.6.30)790-543=

3.6.31)875-461=   3.6.32)882-288=   3.6.33)793-265=   3.6.34)5314-611=   3.6.35)9664-8551=

3.6.36)621-568=   3.6.37)1127-89=   3.6.38)187-129=   3.6.39)327-189=   3.6.40)1321-287=

3.6.41) 571	3.6.42) 2889	3.6.43) 1653	3.6.44) 781	3.6.45) 3256	3.6.46) 321
-343	- 66	-327	-679	-124	-264

3.6.47) 245	3.6.48) 175	3.6.49) 267	3.6.50) 1132	3.6.51) 3199	3.6.52) 127
- 31	-46	- 76	-988	-337	-89

3.6.53)111-2365=   3.6.54)2227-7201=   3.6.55)343-860   3.6.56)165-6825=

3.6.57)8301-9722=   3.6.58)331-602=   3.6.59)1775-1939=   3.6.60)811-483=
3.6.61)6523-105=   3.6.62)376-742=   3.6.63)345-1255=   3.6.64)854-999=
3.6.65)726-855=   3.6.66)116-949=   3.6.67)44-192=   3.6.68)920-1128=
3.6.69)445-3287=   3.6.70)284-8132=   3.6.71)119-855=   3.6.72)336-654=
3.6.73)284-367=   3.6.74)298-727=   3.6.75)29-2259=   3.6.76)119-409=
3.6.77)365-166=   3.6.78)110-627=   3.6.79)475-386=   3.6.80)768-129=

Subtraction Decimals
3.13.1)11-2.3=   3.13.2).22-2.0=   3.13.3)3.4-16=
3.13.4)6.5-6.8=   3.13.5).83-2.2=   3.13.6)3.3-60=
3.13.7)1.7-3.9=   3.13.8)8.1-.48=   3.13.9).65-0.5=
3.13.10)3.7-74=   3.13.11)3.4-2.5=   3.13.12).85-39=
3.13.13).72-35=   3.13.14)1.6-4.9=   3.13.15).44-9.2=
3.13.16)9.2-12=   3.13.17)4.4-.28=   3.13.18)2.8-3.2=
3.13.19)11.1-2.365=   3.13.20)2.227-2.01=   3.13.21)34.3-16.0
3.13.22)16.5-68.25=   3.13.23)83.01-2.2=   3.13.24)3.31-60.2=
3.13.25)1.775-3.9=   3.13.26)81.1-4.83=   3.13.27)65.23-10.5=
3.13.28)37.6-.742=   3.13.29)34.5-25.5=   3.13.30).854-.399=

Adding/Subtraction Complex Signs

3.16.1)-1+2=   3.16.2)-2-2=   3.16.3)-3+1=
3.16.4)6-(-6)=   3.16.5)-8+2=   3.16.6)-3-6=
3.16.7)-1-(-3)=   3.16.8)-8+4=   3.16.9)-6-5=
3.16.10)-3-(-7)=   3.16.11)3-(-2)=   3.16.12)-8+3=
3.16.13)-7-3=   3.16.14)-1-4=   3.16.15)-4-(-9)=
3.16.16)-9+12=   3.16.17)-4-(-2)=   3.16.18) 2-(-3)=
3.16.19)-1-(-2)=   3.16.20)-2-2=   3.16.21)-3+16
3.16.22)-1-(-6)=   3.16.23)-8-2=   3.16.24)-3+6=
3.16.25)-1-3=   3.16.26)-8-(-4)=   3.16.27)-6-1=
3.16.28)-3-7=   3.16.29)-3+2=   3.16.30)-8-(-3)=

3.6.w1) Sue back 827 cookies
        #She sold 127 of the cookies
        #Her brother Mike sold 81 of the cookies
What is the best way to figure out how many cookies she has left over
    a)   827-127-81=, b) 127-827-81=, c) 827+127+81=, d) 127+81-827=
    b)   How many cookies are left over

3.6.w2) Mark picked 427 apples on Monday, the 328 pears on Tues. What is the difference between the number of apples and pears he picked?

3.6.w3)Mike goal is to mow 125 lawns this summer
       # In June he mows 35
       # In July he mows 61
How many lawns must he mow in August to make his goal?

For one on one tutoring via skype at $35.00/Hr.; contact me at marksmathtutoring@yahoo.com

3.6.w38) The table below shows the number of cats and dogs for three different public school

School	Cats	dogs
Harrison	126	217
Casis	118	187
Baker	153	254

What is the total difference between the number of cats and dogs?

3.6.w4)Gilbert bought 87 flowers for his moms garden. He put 31 in the front yard and 27 in the back. How many flowers did he have left?

3.6.w5)Wanda saved the following amount of money in three months
   #March she saved $827
   #April she saved $294
   # May she saved $447
How much more money did she save in March than April and May combined?

3.6.w6)Rita had two boxes of cupcakes
   #She made 85 chocolate
   #She made 76 vanilla
   #Her brother ate 28 of them
Which equation would be useful in finding the number of cupcakes she had left after her brother ate them.
   a) 85+76-28=
   b) 85+76+28=
   c) 85-76+28=
   d) 85-76-28=
   How many cup cakes did she have left after her brother ate some?

3.6.w7) Sarah grew three vegetables in her garden last year. The list below shows the number of each she grew.
   # 127 tomatoes
   # 312 cucumbers
   # 187 carrots
   Which expression below is the best way to determine the difference between the number of carrots and tomatoes she grew?
   a) 127-187, b) 187-127, c) 187+127, d) 127+187

3.6.w8) Mike rode his bike 431 miles in June and 277 mile in July. What is the difference in miles between these two months?

3.6.w9)Larimer save $841 in April, he spent $128 in May then saved another $56 in June. Which expression is best for determining the amount of money he has saved?
   a)841-128+56=
   b) 841-128-56=
   c)841+128+56=
   d)841+56-128=

3.6.w10) Brad has 841 apples in two boxes. He has 367 in one box. How many apples are in the other box?

Croquis of a
Deliberate
Crime

YouTube

3.6.w11) I ate 7 more oranges than apples. Which tables below shows this relationship.

A)

APPLES	ORANGES
4	11
6	13
8	15
10	17
15	24

C)

APPLES	ORANGES
4	11
6	13
8	15
10	17
15	22

B)

APPLES	ORANGES
4	11
6	12
8	15
10	17
15	22

D)

APPLES	ORANGES
4	12
6	14
8	16
10	17
15	22

3.6.w12) If you bake 4 cupcakes on Mon 6 on Tuesday, then 5 on Wednesday, how many cupcakes would you have?

3.6.w13) It took me three years to save $25,357. If the first year I saved $8,113, and $7,891, how much did I save in the third year?

3.6.w14) The table below shows the relationship between the miles I hiking and biking.

MONTH	BIKING	HIKING
June	28	15
July	32	19
August	35	22
September	41	28

Which equation below shows this relationship?
a) Miles biked – 13 = miles hiked
b) Miles biked - 11 = miles hiked
c) Miles biked - 12 = miles hiked
d) Miles biked - 15 = miles hiked

3.6.w15) I have two jars with penny's
Jar A has 27,315 pennies
Jar B has 8,465 pennies
What is the best estimate for the difference in the number of pennies in these two jars?

3.6.w16) I bought a bike to repair then sale. The following is the amount I spent and sold it for
Bought bike for $12.00
Repaired bike for $8.00
#Painted bike for $5.50
#sold bike for $30.00
What is the best estimate for the amount of profit I made?

3.6.w17) You sold pizza at a bake sale. The cost of making all the pizza was $10.35. They sold for a total of $21.11. What was your profit?

3.6.w18) My dog has $14.00 to spend on treats and toys. He buys on ball for $2.85, two cookies for $.65 each, and a chew toy for $1.97. What is the amount of money he has left over?

3.6.w19) The following is a list of the number of miles I walk each month.

#June 327

#July 451

#Aug 634

If my goal was 1500, how many more do I need to walk?

3.6.w20) If the clock below shows the time I stopped watching TV

If I started at 9:15 how long did I watch TV

3.6.w21) If the clock below shows the time I stopped walking

If I started at 11:10 how long did I walk

3.6.w22) The clock below shows the time I stopped playing football.

If I started at 8:10 how many hours and minutes did I play

3.6.w23) The clock below shows the time I stopped playing video games

If I started at 1:15 how long did I play?

3.6.w24) The table below shows the number of cats and dogs for three different public school

School	Cats	dogs
Harrison	126	217
Casis	118	187
Baker	153	254

What is the total difference between the number of cats and dogs?

3.6.w25) My cow weights 125.6 lbs and my sisters cow weights 78.13 lbs. What is the difference in their weights.

3.6.w26) I earned $21.35 for babysitting. I then earned an extra $12.30 for cleaning a house. If I then spent $18.93, what is the total amount I have left over?

3.6.w27) If I buy a hamburger for $8.37 and a coke for $1.87, and I pay with a $20.00 bill what is the change I have left over?

3.6.w28) The table below shows the population in three four different towns.

TOWN	POPULATION
Mercer	11,215
Bellevue	21,561
Tacoma	13,335
Everett	

If the population of Everett is 7,327 less than Bellevue what is the total population of all four towns.

3.6.w29) If I biked 12,348 miles last year and have put a total of 25,668 miles on the bike since buying it last year. How many miles did I bike this year

3.6.w30) The length of two different biking distances are given below.
    # Monday 2.3 Kilometers
    # Tuesday 1250 meters
What is the differences in these distances
a) 1247.7 meters
b) 1252.3 meters
c) 1050 meters
d) 1020 meters

3.6.w31) I need to balance my budget to see how much extra money I have this month. The tables below show my expenses and income

Expenses		Income	
Food	$251.00	Mowing lawns	$342.00
Rent	$450.00	Baby Sitting	$235.00
Utilities	$50.00	House cleaning	$ 578.00

Based on this information how much money do I have left over after expenses?

3.6.w32) If I have a fish 4 meters long and cut it into three pieces. The first is 1.35 meters long, the second is 0.7 meters long, how long is the third piece?

3.6.w33) If I need to be at work at 7.15 a.m. and the drive is 1hour and 30 m minutes long what time should I leave the house?

3.6.w34) If I want to finish doing something at 3:30 and it will take me 2 hours and 45 minutes what time should I start

3.6.w35) If I want to finish walking at 2:15 and it will take me 1 hours and 35 minutes what time should I start

3.6.w36) If I want to finish reading something at 1:30 and it will take me 3 hours and 25 minutes what time should I start

3.6.w37) If I want to finish doing something at 3:30 and it will take me 2 hours and 45 minutes what time should I start

3.6.W38) The table below shows the length and weight of the fish I caught on vacation.

	WEIGHT	LENGTH
BASS	6.8 lbs	13.4 in
TROUT	23.15 lbs	26.78 in

Based on this information which of the following statements is true
A) The combined weights is 29.75 lbs
B) the combined lengths of the fish is 40.18 in
C) The difference in the lengths of the bass and the trout is 16.38 in.
D) The Bass weighed 13.28 pounds less than the trout

3.7 Multiplication-Single Digits

3.7.1) 1x3=   3.7.2) 2x0=   3.7.3) 4x6=   3.7.4) 5x8=   3.7.5) 3x2=   3.7.6) 7x3=
3.7.7) 3x0=   3.7.8) 7x9=   3.7.9) 1x8=   3.7.10) 5x5=   3.7.11) 7x4=   3.7.12) 2x6=
3.7.13) 4x5=   3.7.14) 5x9=   3.7.15) 2x5=   3.7.16) 6x9=   3.7.17) 4x2=   3.7.18) 3x8=
3.7.19) 2x2=   3.7.20) 4x8=   3.7.21) 8x2=   3.7.22) 9x5=   3.7.23) 6x4=   3.7.24) 8x5=
3.7.25) 4x7=   3.7.26) 8x7=   3.7.27) 9x9=   3.7.28) 9x0=   3.7.29) 6x6=   3.7.30) 2x7=
3.7.31) 1x2=   3.7.32) 7x8=   3.7.33) 6x2=   3.7.34) 3x4=   3.7.35) 9x4=   3.7.36) 1x5=
3.7.37) 7x6=   3.7.38) 8x8=   3.7.39) 9x6=   3.7.40) 1x6=   3.7.41) 6x5=   3.7.42) 9x2=

3.7.43) 7 x3	3.7.44) 9 x4	3.7.45) 3 x6	3.7.46) 5 x9	3.7.47) 8 x5	3.7.48) 5 x7

3.7.49) 8 x8	3.7.50) 7 x2	3.7.51) 6 x4	3.7.52) 7 x7	3.7.53) 3 x2	3.7.54) 2 x9

3.8 Multiplication-Two Digits

3.8.1)11x23=   3.8.2)22x20=   3.8.3)34x16=   3.8.4)65x68=   3.8.5)83x22=   3.8.6)33x60=
3.8.7)17x39=   3.8.8)81x48=   3.8.9)65x05=   3.8.10)37x74=   3.8.11)34x25=   3.8.12)85x39=
3.8.13)72x35=   3.8.14)16x49=   3.8.15)44x92=   3.8.16)92x12=   3.8.17)44x28=   3.8.18)28x32=
3.8.19)19x55=   3.8.20)36x54=   3.8.21)84x67=   3.8.22)98x27=   3.8.23)29x59=   3.8.24)19x40=
3.8.25)36x66=   3.8.26)11x62=   3.8.27)47x38=   3.8.28)76x12=   3.8.29)23x64=   3.8.30)79x54=
3.8.31)37x46=   3.8.32)18x88=   3.8.33)79x26=   3.8.34)31x56=   3.8.35)26x85=   3.8.36)84x16=

3.8.37) 21 x34	3.8.38) 57 x56	3.8.39) 89 x32	3.8.40) 65 x67	3.8.41) 81 x83	3.8.42) 27 x53

3.8.43) 45 x31	3.8.44) 75 x46	3.8.45) 67 x76	3.8.46) 32 x88	3.8.47) 99 x37	3.8.48) 56 x78

3.9 Multiple digit Multiplication

3.9.1)111x2365=   3.9.2)2227x201=   3.9.3)343x160   3.9.4)165x6825=
3.9.5)8301x22=   3.9.6)331x602=   3.9.7)1775x39=   3.9.8)811x483=
3.9.9)6523x105=   3.9.10)376x742=   3.9.11)345x255=   3.9.12)854x399=
3.9.13)726x355=   3.9.14)116x949=   3.9.15)44x192=   3.9.16)920x128=
3.9.17)445x287=   3.9.18)284x132=   3.9.19)119x855=   3.9.20)336x254=

3.9.21)284x367=   3.9.22)298x727=   3.9.23)29x2259=   3.9.24)119x409=

3.9.25)365x166=   3.9.26)110x627=   3.9.27)475x386=   3.9.28)768x129=

3.9.29)236x642=   3.9.30)790x543=   3.9.31)375x461=   3.9.32)182x888=

3.9.34)793x265=   3.9.35)314x5611=   3.9.36)2664x8551=   3.9.37)21x568=

3.9.38) 571 x343	3.9.39) 2889 x566	3.90.40)1653 x327	3.9.41) 781 x679	3.9.42) 3256 x124
3.9.43) 245 x31	3.9.44) 175 x46	3.9.45) 267 x376	3.9.46) 132 x988	3.9.47) 199 x337

Multiplication Decimals

3.14.1)11X2.3=   3.14.2).22X2.0=   3.14.3)3.4X16=
3.14.4)6.5X6.8=   3.14.5).83X2.2=   3.14.6)3.3X60=
3.14.7)1.7X3.9=   3.14.8)8.1X.48=   3.14.9).65X0.5=
3.14.10)3.7X74=   3.14.11)3.4X2.5=   3.14.12).85X39=
3.14.13).72X35=   3.14.14)1.6X4.9=   3.14.15).44X9.2=
3.14.16)9.2X12=   3.14.17)4.4X.28=   3.14.18)2.8X3.2=
3.14.19)11.1X2.365=   3.14.20)2.227X2.01=   3.14.21)34.3X16.0
3.14.22)16.5X68.25=   3.14.23)83.01X2.2=   3.14.24)3.31X60.2=
3.14.25)1.775X3.9=   3.14.26)81.1X4.83=   3.14.27)65.23X10.5=
3.14.28)37.6X .742=   3.14.29)34.5X25.5=   3.14.30).854X.399=

The following table details the number of cookies baked on each pan.

Number of cookie pans	Number of cookies
2	12
3	18
4	
6	36
8	48

3.9.w1) How many cookies where baked on 4 pans?
3.9.w2) How many cookies on 7 pans?
3.9.w3) How many cookies on each pan?

3.9.w4) Brad put four turtles in each pond. He has 6 ponds. How many turtle does he have?
3.9.w5) Elizabeth gave 6 rhinos 7 carrots each, how many carrots did she give the rhinos?

Croquis of a
Deliberate
Crime

YouTube

If you don't get the correct answer, and want an explanation on how to work the problem, go to YouTube and type in "MMT" then the problem number. An example would be, MMT 3.9.w12,. The video will show you how to work problem 3.9.w12.

For one on one tutoring via skype at $35.00/Hr.; contact me at marksmathtutoring@yahoo.com

3.9.w6) There are four pairs of socks in each package. Which table below shows the relationship between the number of socks and the number of packages.

a)

Number of Packages	4	5	6	8
Number of Socks	12	15	18	21

b)

Number of Packages	4	5	6	8
Number of Socks	16	18	20	22

c)

Number of Packages	4	5	6	8
Number of Socks	16	20	24	32

d)

Number of Packages	4	5	6	8
Number of Socks	1	13	24	35

3.9.w7) There are two different types of cupcakes for sale
5 boxes with 6 chocolate cupcakes in each
there are 42 vanilla cup cakes on the table
What is the total number of cupcakes on sale?

3.9.w8) What number goes in the box to make the mathematical statement true $\bigcirc$X6=42

3.9.w9) The baseball team bought 7 boxes of candy bars to sell. Each box has 9 candy bars in them. How many bars do they have to sell?

3.9.w10) In the equations below, the Δ always represents the same number.
$\square$ + Δ = 8
Δ X Δ = 4
What is the value of $\square$?

3.9.w11) The following table describes the number of potatoes in a bag.

Number of bags	1	4	6	7
Number of Potatoes	15	60		105

Each bag has the same number of potatoes in it. How many potatoes are in 6 bags?
a) 45, because 105-60=45
b) 90, because 6X15=90
c) 45, because 60-15=45
d) 75, because 15+60=75

3.9.w12) At the bakery the cupcakes are in boxes with 12 cupcakes each. If you count in groups of 12 which numbers will you use?
a) 12, 24, 38, 42
b) 10, 20, 30, 40
c) 12, 24, 36, 48
d) 36, 48, 59, 61

3.9.W13) The table below show the total number of horses for different number of stalls

Number of stalls	1	3	5	7
Number of Horses	5	15		35

There is a equal number of horses in each stall. Which equation is the best way to determine the number if horses in 5 stalls?
a) 3+15=, b) 5X15=, c) 5+15=, d) 5X5=

3.9.w14) You made cupcakes for your school and put them in 8 boxes. There are 73 cupcakes in each box. How many cupcakes did you make.

3.9.w15) The table below show the total number of apples in different number of bags

Number of bags	1	2	3	5
Number of apples	12	24		60

There is a equal number of apples in each bag. How many apples are in 3 bags?

3.9.w16) The school sells 96 cookies every day. How many cookies will they sell in 8 days?

3.9.w17) There are 28 apple pies, and 17 peach pies. Each is for sale for $7.00. How much money will it take to buy all of the pies?

3.9.w18) The table below lists the number of rabbits in different number of cages.

Number of cages	Number of rabbits
3	12
5	20
7	28
8	
10	40

Each cage contains the same number of rabbits. What is one way to determine the number of rabbits in 8 cages
    a) find the difference between 40 and 28
    b) find the product of 8X4
    c) find the sum of 40 and 28
    d)find the difference between 40 and 10.

3.9.w19) The table below shows the number of people that enter a public bus each hour.

Number of hours	Number of people
1	16
2	32
4	
5	80
8	128

Each hour the same number of people enter the bus. How many people entered the bus in 5 hours?
a) 48, because 128-80=48
b) 64, because 4X16=64
c) 48, because 32+16=48
d) 16, because 32÷16=2

3.9.w20) While on a field trip to the ocean, 5 kids collect 15 shells each, which expression can be used to determine the total number of shells collected?
    a) 15÷5=
    b) 15X5=
    c) 15+5=
    d) 15-5=
How many shells in total where collected?

Croquis of a
Deliberate
Crime
YouTube

3.9.w21) The table below shows the total number of kids in different number of buses.

Number of buses	Number of Kids
2	24
5	60
6	
7	84
9	108

Each bus has the same number of kids in it. How many kids total will be in 6 buses?

3.9.w22) Andy practices math 2 hours a day. How many hours will he practice in 9 days?

3.9.w23) Michelle practices math 3 hours a day, and history 2 hours a day. What is the total number of hours in 7 days she practices?

3.9.w24) Emery drew 6 rows of dogs. Each row has 8 dogs in it. How many dogs did she draw?

3.9.w25) The table below shows the number of dogs of different colors.

Color of Dog	Number of Dogs
Black	48
Yellow	32
Brown	24
Spotted	56

The picture graph below represents the same information

Color of Dogs	Number of Dogs
Black	X X X X X X
Yellow	X X X X
Brown	X X X
Spotted	X X X X X X X

Which Key completes the picture graph?
a) Each X means 6 dogs
b) Each X means 8 dogs
c) Each X means 4 dogs
d) Each X means 2 dogs.

3.9.w26) John has 16 packages a baseball cards. Each pack has 6 cards in it. He gives 12 to a friend. Which mathematical stamen below will help determine the amount of cards he has left?
a) 16x12-6=186
b) 16x6-12=84
c) 12+6+16=34
d) 12X6-16=56

Croquis of a
Deliberate
Crime

YouTube

If you don't get the correct answer, and want an explanation on how to work the problem, go to YouTube and type in "MMT" then the problem number. An example would be, MMT 3.9.w12,. The video will show you how to work problem 3.9.w12.

3.9.w27) I eat 4 apple a day. Which table below describes the number of apples total I have eaten in 4, 6, 7 days

A)

NUMBER OF DAYS	TOTAL NUMBER OF APPLES
4	16
6	24
7	28

C)

NUMBER OF DAYS	TOTAL NUMBER OF APPLES
4	16
6	22
7	28

B)

NUMBER OF DAYS	TOTAL NUMBER OF APPLES
4	16
6	24
7	26

D)

NUMBER OF DAYS	TOTAL NUMBER OF APPLES
4	18
6	24
7	28

3.9.w28) If a restaurant charges $6.00 per meal which table below describes the cost for a specific number of meals

A)

Number of Meals	4	5	7	9
Total Cost of Meals	$24	$30	$44	$54

C)

Number of Meals	4	5	7	9
Total Cost of Meals	$24	$30	$42	$54

B)

Number of Meals	4	5	7	9
Total Cost of Meals	$24	$28	$42	$48

D)

Number of Meals	4	5	7	9
Total Cost of Meals	$26	$28	$42	$52

3.9.w29) I sold pies at a rate of $7.00 per pie. Which tables below show this relationship?

A)

NUMBER OF PIES	TOTAL COST
2	$14
4	$26
6	$42
7	$49
8	$56

C)

NUMBER OF PIES	TOTAL COST
2	$14
4	$28
6	$42
7	$49
8	$56

B)

NUMBER OF PIES	TOTAL COST
2	$14
4	$28
6	$42
7	$48
8	$56

D)

NUMBER OF PIES	TOTAL COST
2	$14
4	$32
6	$42
7	$48
8	$56

3.9.w30) My sister put 3 apples and 4 oranges in each lunch bag. There are 8 lunch bags. What is the total number of pieces of fruit.

Croquis of a
Deliberate
Crime

YouTube

If you don't get the correct answer, and want an explanation on how to work the problem, go to YouTube and type in "MMT" then the problem number. An example would be, MMT 3.9.w12,. The video will show you how to work problem 3.9.w12.

For one on one tutoring via skype at $35.00/Hr.; contact me at marksmathtutoring@yahoo.com

3.9.w31) Given the mathematical statement below.

◇ X 10 = ◯

Which table below represents this relationship

a)

◇	◯
26	36
34	44
57	67
69	79

c)

◇	◯
26	260
34	340
57	570
69	690

b)

◇	◯
26	27
34	35
57	58
69	70

d)

◇	◯
26	2.6
34	3.4
57	5.7
69	6.9

3.9.w32) Your soccer team plays 16 games a year. How many games will they play in 24 years?

3.9.w33) Each box has 16 rocks in it. If there are 37 boxes how many rocks total are there?

3.9.w34) If you sell boxes of cookies. The table below shows the number of cookies in each box.

BOXES	27	35	69	121
COOKIES	2,700	3,500		12,100

How many cookies will be in 69 boxes?

3.9.w35) If you mow 6 lawns a day, 7 days a week for 8 weeks and earn $12.00 per lawn how much money have you earned?

3.9.w36) Given the numerical sequence shown below
 18, 21, 24, 27
Which of the tables below shows this relationship

a)

NUMBER	RELATIONSHIP	ANSWER
17	17+1	18
20	20+1	21
23	23+1	24
26	26+1	27

c)

NUMBER	RELATIONSHIP	ANSWER
18	18+0	18
21	21+0	21
24	24+0	24
27	27+0	27

b)

NUMBER	RELATIONSHIP	ANSWER
6	6X3=	18
7	7X3=	21
8	8X3=	24
9	9X3=	27

d)

NUMBER	RELATIONSHIP	ANSWER
18	18X1=	18
21	21X1=	21
24	24X1=	24
27	27X1=	27

3.9.w37) There are 36 kids in a class rooom. There are 25 class rooms. How many kids in this school?

3.9.w38) If I put 100 cupcakes in each box and there are 48 boxes, how many cupcakes do I have?

For one on one tutoring via skype at $35.00/Hr.; contact me at marksmathtutoring@yahoo.com

3.9.w39) Given the numerical relationship shown below

$\diamondsuit$ **X 15 =** $\bigcirc$

Which table below best describes this relationship.

a)

$\diamondsuit$	2	4	6	8
$\bigcirc$	17	19	21	23

c)

$\diamondsuit$	2	4	6	8
$\bigcirc$	13	11	9	7

b)

$\diamondsuit$	2	4	6	8
$\bigcirc$	15	30	45	60

d)

$\diamondsuit$	2	4	6	8
$\bigcirc$	30	60	90	120

3.9.w40) It cost $14.00 to paint a bike. The following list details how many bikes I painted
Thursday I painted 337 bikes
Friday I painted 181 bikes
Saturday I painted 257 bikes
What is the total cost of painting these bikes?

3.9.w41) The following table shows the number of apples in each pie.

NUMBER OF PIES	NUMBER OF APPLES
1	32
2	64
3	96
4	128

Which of the following equations best described this relationship
a) total number of pies + 31 = total number of apples
b) total number of pies X 32 = total number of apples
c) total number of pies ÷ 31 = total number of apples
d) total number of pies - 31 = total number of apples

3.9.w42) If I throw the ball for my dog 34 times a day for 56 days. How many times have I thrown the ball for him?

3.9.w43) A season pass for the movie theater cost $100. If 125 people buy one how much money did the theater make?

3.9.w44) There are 49 boxes of light bulbs. Each box has 24 bulbs in it. What is the total number of light bulbs?

3.9.w45) If I buy 6 boxes of cookies and each has 8 cookies in it. What is the total number of cookies I have bought?

3.9.w46) I put the same number of chocolate chips in each cookie, and the relationship[describing how many each cookie gets is described in the table below.

NUMBER OF COOKIES	20	25	30	35
NUMBER OF CHIPS	300	375	450	525

Which of the following equations below describes this relationship?
a) Number of Cookies + 250 = Number of Chips
b) Number of Cookies - 250 = Number of Chips
c) Number of Cookies X 15 = Number of Chips
d) Number of Cookies ÷ 15 = Number of Chips

3.9.w47) Given the drawing below

Which of the following boxes would have the same number of squares in it?

a)   c)

b)   d)

3.9.w48) There are 420 tress in a orchards. Which of the following equations can describe the shape of the orchard?
a) 7 rows of 70 tress = 420
b) 6 rows of 70 tress = 420
c) 8 rows of 54 tress = 420
d) 9 rows of 50 trees = 420

3.9.w49) Which table below best describes the relationship Y = 4 X

A)

X	Y
3	9
5	20
6	24
8	32

B)

X	Y
3	12
5	15
6	24
8	32

C)

X	Y
3	12
5	20
6	24
8	28

D)

X	Y
3	12
5	20
6	24
8	32

3.9.W50) What is the total if I subtract 27 from the product of 23 and 17

3.9.W51) On Monday I caught 31 fish, and on Tues I caught 127 fish. If each fish weighs 8 pounds how much in pounds did I catch between the two days.

3.9.W52) If I bike 25 miles a week for 5 weeks what is the total distance?

3.9.w53) I measured the weights all the dogs in my neighborhood. 27 weighted 18 pounds and 13 weighted 27 pounds. What is the total weight of these dogs?

3.9.W54) The table below shows the process of admittance to a theme park

TYPE OF ADMISSION	ADULT	CHILD
GENERAL ADMISSION	$12.00	$10.00
SPECIAL	$10.00	$8.00
OFF SEASSON	$7.00	$5.00
LATE NIGHT	$9.00	$7.00

Based on this information if I bought 2 adult tickets and three child tickets and payed a total of $29.00, what kind of tickets did I buy?

3.9.w55) If I play video games at the arcade for $1.25 per hour, for 3 hours a day and for 5 days how much money did I spend?

3.9.w56) I pet 321 dogs a year, for 32 years. What is the total amount of dogs I pet?

3.9.w57) If I eat 3.7 pounds of fish a month for 1.3 months how many pounds of fish have I eaten.

3.9.w58) Which of the following table best described the relationship y = 0.15 X

A)

X	Y
5	50
10	100
15	150
20	200
25	250

B)

X	Y
5	75
10	150
15	175
20	300
25	325

C)

X	Y
5	.75
10	1.50
15	1.75
20	3.00
25	3.25

D)

X	Y
5	.075
10	.150
15	.175
20	.300
25	.325

3.9.W59) I have 139 cookies in the kitchen then add 28 more boxes. Each box has 24 cookies in it. What is the total number of cookies in the kitchen?

3.9.w60) If it take me 1:45 to mow a single lawn and I have 3 to do, how much time will it take.

3.9.w61) If it take 45 minutes to bake a sheet of cookies and I have 5 sheets, how much time will it take

3.9.w62) If I it take 35 minutes to wash a car and I have 6 to do, and I start at 2:15 what time will I be done

3.9.w63) To walk a dog takes 1hour and 45 minutes. If I have 5 dogs to walk how much time will it take.

3.10 Division-no remainders

3.10.1) 2÷1= 3.10.2) 2÷2= 3.10.3) 3÷1= 3.10.4) 3÷3= 3.10.5) 4÷1= 3.10.6) 4÷2=
3.10.7) 4÷4= 3.10.8) 5÷1= 3.10.9) 5÷5= 3.10.10) 6÷1= 3.10.11) 6÷2= 3.10.12) 6÷3=
3.10.13) 6÷6= 3.10.14) 7÷1= 3.10.15) 7÷7= 3.10.16) 8÷1= 3.10.17) 8÷2= 3.10.18) 8÷4=
3.10.19) 8÷8= 3.10.20) 9÷1= 3.10.21) 9÷3= 3.10.22) 9÷9= 3.10.23) 10÷1= 3.10.24) 10÷2=
3.10.25) 10/5= 3.10.26) 10/10= 3.10.27) 12/1= 3.10.28) 12/2= 3.10.29) 12/3= 3.10.30) 12/4=
3.10.31) 12/6= 3.10.32) 12/12= 3.10.33) 14/1= 3.10.34) 14/2= 3.10.35) 14/7= 3.10.36) 14/14=
3.10.37) 15/1= 3.10.38) 15/3= 3.10.39) 15/5= 3.10.40) 15/15= 3.10.41) 18/3= 3.10.42) 18/6=

3.10.43) 20   3.10.44) 9   3.10.45) 6   3.10.46) 15   3.10.47) 8   3.10.48) 10
       ÷2   ÷3   ÷2   ÷5   ÷4   ÷2

3.10.49) 8   3.10.50) 8   3.10.51) 6   3.10.52) 7   3.10.53) 8   3.10.54) 2
       ÷8   ÷2   ÷3   ÷7   ÷2   ÷2

3.10.55) 136÷4=   3.10.56) 180÷5=   3.10.57) 64÷2=   3.10.58)112÷4=
3.10.59)280÷5=   3.10.60) 364÷7=   3.10.61) 488÷8=   3.10.62) 141÷3=
3.10.63)477÷9=   3.10.64) 232÷4=   3.10.65) 208÷8=   3.10.66) 267÷3=
3.10.67)581÷7=   3.10.68)455÷5=   3.10.69)86÷2=   3.10.70)312÷6=
3.10.71) 162÷2=   3.10.72) 192÷3=   3.10.73) 576÷9=   3.10.74) 536÷8=
3.10.75) 476÷7=   3.10.76)1840÷5=   3.10.77)1944÷9=   3.10.78) 72÷3=

3.10.79) 56/2=   3.10.80) 76/4=   3.10.81) 156/6=   3.10.82) 360/8=
3.10.83) 405/9=   3.10.84) 399/7=   3.10.85) 184/4=   3.10.86) 1296/6=
3.10.87) 128/8=   3.10.88) 651/7=   3.10.89) 370/5=   3.10.90) 156/3=
3.10.91) 894/6=   3.10.92) 130/5=   3.10.93) 112/2=   3.10.94)105/3=
3.10.95) 846/9=   3.10.96) 672/8=   3.10.97) 7784/7= 3.10.98) 4452/4=
3.10.99) 186/2=   3.10.100) 210/6= 3.10.101) 54/3=   3.10.102) 272/8=
3.10.103) 160/5= 3.10.104) 147/7= 3.10.105) 752/8= 3.10.106) 684/9=
3.10.108) 252/7= 3.10.109) 1435/5= 3.10.110) 140/4= 3.10.111) 134/2=

3.10.113) 4√544   3.10.114) 5√320   3.10.115) 7√2002   3.10.116) 9√1143

3.10.117) 8√1896   3.10.118) 3√51   3.10.119) 9√522   3.10.120) 6√1164

3.10.121) 7√546   3.10.122) 5√305   3.10.123) 3√186   3.10.124) 4√188

3.10.125) 8√768   3.10.126) 4√1132   3.10.127) 6√282   3.10.128) 7√252

3.10.129) 7√364   3.10.130) 6√510   3.10.131) 4√1132   3.10.132) 9√423

3.10.133) 3√81   3.10.134) 7√693   3.10.135) 3√123   3.10.136) 8√1184

3.10.137) 4√196   3.10.138) 9√288   3.10.139) 5√2430   3.10.140) 6√1164

3.10.141) 4√52   3.10.142) 9√756   3.10.143) 8√96   3.10.144) 5√185

Decimals
Round to the nearest tenths place

3.15.1)11÷2.3=   3.15.2).22÷2.0=   3.15.3)3.4÷16=
3.15.4)6.5÷6.8=   3.15.5).83÷2.2=   3.15.6)3.3÷60=
3.15.7)1.7÷3.9=   3.15.8)8.1÷.48=   3.15.9).65÷0.5=

Round to the nearest hundredths place

3.15.10)3.7÷74=   3.15.11)3.4÷2.5=   3.15.12).85÷39=
3.15.13).72÷35=   3.15.14)1.6÷4.9=   3.15.15).44÷9.2=
3.15.16)9.2÷12=   3.15.17)4.4÷.28=   3.15.18)2.8÷3.2=

Multiplication/Division Complex

3.17.1)(21)X(-3)=   3.17.2)(-9)X(-3)=   3.17.3)(26)X(-1)=
3.17.4)(-6)X(-6)=   3.17.5)(-83)X(2)=   3.17.6)(-3)X(-60)=
3.17.7)(-1)X(-3.9)=   3.17.8) (8)X(-4)=   3.17.9)(-6)X(5)=
3.17.10)(-3)X(-7)=   3.17.11)(-3)X(2)=   3.17.12)(85)X(-3)=
3.17.13)(72)X(-3)=   3.17.14)(-1)X(-4)=   3.17.15)(4)X(-9)=
3.17.16)(9)÷(-1)=   3.17.17)(-4)÷(-2)=   3.17.18)(2)÷(-1)=
3.17.19)(-1)÷(1)=   3.17.20)(-6)÷(-2)=   3.17.21)(3)÷(-3)
3.17.22)(-8)÷(-4)=   3.17.23)(2)÷(-2)=   3.17.24)(-9)÷(-3)=
3.17.25)(-16)÷(8)=   3.17.26)(-81)÷(-9)=   3.17.27)(65)÷(-5)=

3.10.w1) thru 3.10.w3) The picture blow shows how many flowers Sarah bought to put in her garden.

She will plant them in rows of 8 flowers.
3.10.w1) How many rows will she have once completed?
3.10.w2) How many rows will have 4 flowers?
3.10.w3) How many flowers are not in a row of 4 flowers?

3.10.w4) Mike has 15 tomatoes to but on 5 hamburgers. He wants to deposit the same amount of tomatoes on each burger. How many does each hamburger get?

3.10.w5) Mrs. Garcia has 42 cups. She wants to put them in 6 boxes each with the same amount of cups. How many cups does each box have?

3.10.w6) Aaron will place 45 rocks from his collection on a self. Each shelf will have 9 rocks. How many selves does he need?

3.10.w7) 6 students from your school go to the zoo with 11 carrots each. They want to feed 3 animals with equal number of carrots. Which equation is the best way to figure out how many carrots each animal will get.
a) 6X11÷3= b) 6X2÷11=, c) 2X11÷6=, d) 2X11X6=

3.10.w8) The bicycle shop has 42 bike for sale. They are arranged into 6 rows with an even number of bikes in each row. How many bikes are there in each row?

3.10.w9) The picture bellows shows the number of bike at a store.

The bike will be arranged in three rows with the same number in each. Which expression below will determine the number of bikes in each row.
a) 6, because 18÷3=6, b) 8, because 15÷3+3=8, c) 5, because 15÷3=5, d) 3, because 15÷5=3

3.10.w10) The band director has 28 trumpets

He will put a same number of trumpets on 7 selves. How many trumpets will be on each self?
a) 8, because 28÷7=8
b) 4, because 28÷7=4
c) 7, because 28÷4=7
d) 4, because 28÷7=7

3.10.w11) The candle shown below will be arranged in 4 rows.

Each row will have the same number of candles. Which mathematical express is best for determining the number of candles in each row?
a) 20÷4=5
b) 10÷5=2
c) 20÷5=4
d) 10÷2=5

3.10.W12) Nellie is putting on a dog show in her neighborhood. There are 16 dogs entered as shown below.

If she puts the dogs into 4 rows, Each row has the same number of dogs. How many dogs will be in each row?
a) 12, 16÷4=12
b) 4, 16÷4=4
c) 3, 6÷3=2
d) 8, 16÷2=8

3.10.w13) Verna bought 20 trees for his farm, as shown below.

He wants to plant them in 5 rows. Each row will have the same number of trees in it. Which mathematical expression will help in determining the number of trees in each row?
a) 20X4=100
b) 4X6=24
c) 20÷5=4
d) 20÷2=10

3.10.w14) Danielle sorted 40 greeting cards into 5 equally sized groups. Which statement below is **NOT** in the same fact family as 40÷5=8
a) 8X5=40
b) 5X4=8
c) 40÷8=5
d) 5X8=40

3.10.w15) John has 14 model boat to play with, as shown below.

While playing with them in the bath, he arranges them in 2 rows with equal number in each. Which statement below will help determine the number of boats in each row?
a) 14÷2=7
b) 2X14=28
c) 14-2=10
d) 14÷7=2

3.10.w16) I put 36 dozen cookies into 4 boxes. If each box has an even number of cookies how many cookies does each box have?

3.10.w17) I have 138 trees places in 6 rows. Each row has the same number of trees. How many trees are in each row?

3.10.w18) If I have 128 cupcakes to put into boxes. Each box can hold 8 cupcakes. How many boxes do I need.
a) 15, b) 16, c) 17, d) 8

3.10.w19) If I have 24 horses and put 6 hoarse in each field. How many fields will I need?
a) 3, b) 4, c) 6, d) 23

3.10.w20) I have 146 pennies. I will stack them in groups of 8. How many stacks will I have?
a) 17, b)18, c)19, d)20

3.10.w21) If I have 35 dollars to but hamburgers. Each burger is 6 dollars. How many burgers can I buy?
a) 4, b) 5, c) 6, d) 7

3.10.w22) The table below show the number of feet in a given number of yards

NUMBER OF YARDS	NUMBER OF FEET
33	11
12	4
42	14
81	27

Which of the following equations best represents this relationship
a)Number of Yards – 21 = Number of feet
b)Number of Yards X 2 = Number of feet
c)Number of Yards – 8 = Number of feet
d)Number of Yards ÷ 3= Number of feet

3.10.w23) The table below show the number of fluid ounces in a given number of teaspoons

NUMBER OF TEASPOONS	NUMBER OF FLUID OUNCES
34	17
12	6
42	21
82	42

Which of the following equations best represents this relationship
a)Number of Teaspoons – 17 = Number of Fluid Ounces
b) Number of Teaspoons – 6 = Number of Fluid Ounces
c) Number of Teaspoons ÷ 6 = Number of Fluid Ounces
d) Number of Teaspoons ÷ 2 = Number of Fluid Ounces

3.10.w24) If I jog 108 minutes over 4 days. The same amount of time each day. How many minutes did I jog each day.

3.10.w25 There are 216 students in a school. They are divided evenly between 9 class. How many are in each class?

3.10.w26) You teacher orders apples to make pies. Each pie gets the same number of apples
There are 32 pies.
each pie gets 45 apples
#The apples are divided evenly between 8 boxes
How many apples are in each box?

3.10.w27) If the 6 elephants at the zoo eat a total 204 bananas, and each one ate the same amount, how many bananas did each elephant get to eat?

3.10.w28) You bought 34 cases of carrots for a trip to the zoo. Each case had 25 carrots each. If five rhino divided the carrots evenly how many did each one get?

3.10.w29) If I have 128 cookies to divide into piles of three cookies each. How many piles do I have?

3.10.w30) I have a bunch of toys. I divided them into 2 equal groups. Which equation can **NOT** be used to find the number of toys in each group.
a) ⃝÷2=5
b) 2+5=⃝
c) 2X5=⃝
d) 5x2=⃝

3.10.w31) I buy a computer and 3 video games for $560. If I spent $389 for the computer and the same amount for each video game, how much did each game cost?

3.10.w32) The following table shows how many pennies were in five different boxes

BOX	NUMBER OF PENNIES
A	87
B	24
C	56
D	76
E	17

If I divide the pennies into 4 equal piles, how many pennies will be in each group?

3.10.w33) I had 147 strawberries. If I divide them into 7 equal piles, how many are in each?

3.10.w34) Which diagram below represents the equation 27÷3?

a)

XXXX
XXXX
XXXX
XXXX
XXXX
XXXX

c)

XXXXXXXXX
XXXXXXXXX
XXXXXXXXX

b)

XXXXXXX⃝
XXXXXXX
XXXXXXX
XXXXXXX

d)

XXXXXX⃝
XXXXXX⃝
XXXXXX⃝
XXXXX
XXXXX

3.10.w35) The table below show a mathematical relationship

⃝	Δ
25	5
15	3
40	8
10	2

Which of the following below best represents this relationship?
a) Δ - 20 = ⃝
b) Δ ÷ 4 = ⃝
c) Δ + 20 = ⃝
d) Δ X 5 = ⃝

3.10.w36) In the equation below the $\bigcirc$ and the $\triangle$ represent different numbers

$$\bigcirc X \triangle = 42$$

Which of the following is in the same fact family

a) $42 X \bigcirc = \triangle$

b) $\triangle X 42 = \bigcirc$

c) $42 \div \bigcirc = \triangle$

d) $\bigcirc \div \triangle = 42$

3.10.w37) I have 725 cookies. I separate them into 5 groups of equal amounts. How many cookies will be in two of the groups.

a) 145

b) 290

c) 730

d) 435

3.10.w38) I paid $76.20 for a magazine subscription that last 12 months. What is the cost of each issue?

3.10.w39) If I saved $187.50 over 5 weeks. If I saved the same amount each week how much did I save each week

3.10.w40) If I have 49 cupcakes that weight 2352 grams. How much does each cupcake weight if each has the same weight.

3.10.w41) The following number all have something in common. { 12, 126, 411, 873}

A) They are divisible by 4

B) They are divisible by 6

C) They are divisible by 3

D) They are divisible by 2

3.10.W42) The following table describes how many cupcakes I have vs the number of boxes.

CUPCAKES	BOXES
51	3
85	5
119	7
136	8

Which statement below is true about the relationship shown above

A) The number of boxes plus 28 equals the number of cupcakes

B) The number of cupcakes minus 28 equals the number of boxes

C) The number of cupcakes times 17 equals the number of boxes

D) The number of cupcakes divided by 17 equals the number of boxes

3.10.w43) If I have 864 pennies I want to put into 36 rows each with the same number of pennies. How many rows will I have.

3.10.w44) While going fishing I had 204 worms. I used 36 of them then divided the remaining evenly between 4 friends. Which equation below would be best to determine how many worms each friend received.

A) (204-36)x4=N

B) (204-36)-4=N

C) (204-36)÷4=N

D) (204-36) + 4=N

3.10.w45) What is the quotient when 0.93 is divided by 3

3.10.w46) I have 1995 fish to divide evenly between 15 tanks. How many fish will be in each tank.

3.10.w47) I have a rope 4.27 feet long. I cut it into 7 equal parts. How long is each in inches

3.10.w48) If I have 429 cupcakes and want to put 13 in a box. How many boxes will I need.

3.10.w49) If I buy a car for $1100.08 and makes 8 equal sized payments, what is the amount of each payment.

3.10.w50) If I have 508 can of soda and want to put them on four shelves in equal amounts. How many cans will be on each shelve.

3.10.w51) If I mowed 5 lawns in 4 hours and 35 minutes, how long did each lawn take

3.10.w52) If it took me 3 hours and 30 minutes to bake 6 sheet of cookies how long did it tale to bake each sheet

3.10.w53) If it take me 7 hours to do 4 jobs how long was each job

3.10.w54) If I walk 5 miles in 5 hours and 25 minutes than how long did each mile take
3.10.w55) If I have 45 pennies and I place them in stacks of 7, how many stacks of 7 do I have
3.10.w56) If I have 36 pennies and I place them in stacks of 7, how many stacks total do I have
3.10.w57) If I have 37 pennies and I place them in stacks of 5, how many stacks of 5 do I have
3.10.w58) If I have 61 pennies and I place them in stacks of 9, how many stacks total do I have
3.10.w59) If I have 24 pennies and I place them in stacks of 9, how many stacks of 9 do I have
3.10.w60) If I have 27 pennies and I place them in stacks of 4, how many stacks of 4 do I have
3.10.w61) If I have 12 pennies and I place them in stacks of 5, how many stacks of 5 do I have
3.10.w62) If I have 83 pennies and I place them in stacks of 5, how many stacks of 5 do I have

3.11 Inequalities
State if these are true or false

3.11.1) 3<1 3.11.2) 5>5 3.11.3) 7$\leq$7 3.11.4) 14<7 3.11.5) 56<81 3.11.6) 4>8
3.11.7) 81<45 3.11.8) 85$\geq$51 3.11.9) 3<9 3.11.10) 43>67 3.11.11) 2<8 3.11.12) 41<41
3.11.13) 76$\leq$76 3.11.14) 78<98 3.11.15) 8<4 3.11.16) 9$\leq$12 3.11.17) 76$\leq$67 3.11.18) 543>73
3.11.19) 0<1 3.11.20) 13<7 3.11.21) 67>43 3.11.22) 13$\geq$31 3.11.23)45<45 3.11.24) 123>237

3.11.25) 3.01<-3.10 3.11.26) 5.0>-5.00 3.11.27) 7.11$\leq$-71.1 3.11.28) -14.30<7.30

3.11.29) 4.15>4.25 3.11.30) 5.167<5.168 3.11.31) 7.2456>7.3345 3.11.32) 2.34<2.24
3.11.33) 5.551<5.450 3.11.34) 6.28>6.38 3.11.35) 1.25>1.26 3.11.36) 4.445>4.545
3.11.37) 6.01>6.010 3.11.38) 8.291<8.190 3.11.39) 3.24>3.25 3.11.40) 6.01$\geq$6.010
3.11.41) 4.556>4.555 3.11.42) 3.6>2.65 3.11.43) 6.779<6.778 3.11.44)7.3>8.2
3.11.45) 8.667<8.668 3.11.46) 7.89<7.88 3.11.47) 2.356>2.365 3.11.48) 3.225>3.252

3.11.49)-6.45<-5.45 3.11.50) -3.56<-3.66 3.11.51)-1.235<-1.236 3.11.52) -7.68<-7.58
3.11.53) -9.551<-9.550 3.11.54) -5.67<-5.68 3.11.55) -5.336>-5.363 3.11.56)-6.344>-6.343
3.11.57) -3.778>-3.768 3.11.58)6.00$\leq$6.0 3.11.59) –4.25<-4.26 3.11.60) -9.446>-9.436
3.11.61) -6.67<-6.87 3.11.62) -7.667>-7.578 3.11.63)-5.01>-5.10 3.11.64) -4.326<-4.437
3.11.65)-3.11>-31.1 3.11.66) -4.01<-4.10 3.11.67) -7.89>-7.81 3.11.68) -5.6>-4.7
3.11.69) -66.8>-69.4 3.11.70) -3.45<-3.450 3.11.71)-2.34>-2.36 3.11.72) -89.90<-89.901

3.11.w1) A group of number is shown below

| 2467 | 2586 | 2775 | 2911 |

Which statement below is true:
a) 2586 >2476 because the 5>4.
b) 2467>2911 because 67>11
c) 2775>2467 because 75 is greater than 67
d) 2467<2586 because 67<86

3.11.w2) A groups of number is shown below

| 137 | 366 | 415 | 110 |

Which statement below is true
a) 415<366 because 66<15
b) 137>415 because 37 is greater than 15
c) 366>415 because 6>5
d) 110<366 because 1<3

3.11.w3) A group of numbers is shown below

| 4 | 8 | 9 | 5 |

Which statement below is **NOT** true
a) 4<8
b)9>4
c) 9>8
d)4>9

3.11.w4) A group of numbers is shown below

| 827 | 199 | 1127 | 531 |

Which statement below is true
a) 827>1127 because the 8 > 11
b) 199>531 because 1>5
c) 531>1127 because 53>11
d) 1127>827 because 1>0

3.11.w5) The following list shows three clues about a number I am thinking about.
the number is greater than 3578
the number is less than 5587
There is a 6 in the hundreds place
Which of the following could be this number
a) 6156
b) 4729
c) 4699
d)2687

3.11.w6) The following list shows three clues about a number I am thinking about.
the number is greater than 379
the number is less than 421
There is a 8 in the tens place
Which of the following could be this number
a) 581
b) 381
c) 289
d)417

3.11.w7) The following list shows three clues about a number I am thinking about.
the number is greater than 28
the number is less than 54
There is a 7 in the ones place
Which of the following could be this number
a) 42
b) 73
c) 47
d)31

3.11.w8) The sum of 6 thousands 4 hundreds 5 tens and 2 ones is which of the following
a) 6542
b) 2546
c)6452
d) 17

3.11.w9) The sum of 8 thousands 3 hundreds 0 tens and 1 ones is which of the following
a) 8031
b) 1038
c) 8301
d) 12

3.11.w10) I have 12.25 pounds of potatoes and my friend has 15.7 pounds. Which number below is between these two numbers.
A) 11.37, B) 16.80, C) 12.37, D) 3.45

Croquis of a
Deliberate
Crime
YouTube

If you don't get the correct answer, and want an explanation on how to work the problem, go to YouTube and type in "MMT" then the problem number. An example would be, MMT 3.9.w12,. The video will show you how to work problem 3.9.w12.

For one on one tutoring via skype at $35.00/Hr.; contact me at marksmathtutoring@yahoo.com

4 GEOMETRY

4.1) Which of the following is not a Rhombus, trapezoid, rectangle or square?

4.2) Which of the following is not a polygon?

4.3) Which of the following figures is not a quadrilateral?

4.4) Which of the following is not a Rhombus, trapezoid, rectangle or square?

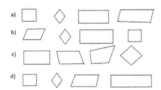

4.5) Which statement is true about the following figures?

a) All the figures are Rhombuses
b) All the figures are polygons
c) All the figures are parallelograms
d) All figures are Quadrilaterals

4.61) Which of the following is required for a pentagon?
a) right angles
b) parallel lines
c) 4 vertices
d) five sides

Croquis of a
Deliberate
Crime

YouTube

4.62) The following figures share a common characteristic.

a) all are trapezoids
b) all are squares
c) all are triangles
d) all are quadrilaterals

4.39) Which of the following figure is not a pentagon

4.40) Which of the following figure is not a hexagon

4.81) Which of the following is a rectangle?

4.6) Which figure has symmetry

4.7) Which figure does not have symmetry

4.65) The drawing below is only half of the figure. The rest of it is a symmetry about the line AB

Which one of the following could complete this figure
a)   b)

c)   d)

4.66) Which drawing below has two lines of symmetry?

A) B) C) D)

4.67) Which of the drawings below has only one line of symmetry?

A) B) C) D)

4.68) Which of the following figures has both a horizontal and a vertical line of symmetry?

A) B) C) D)

4.69) Which figure below has only a horizontal line of symmetry, no vertical?

A) B) C) D)

4.70) Which figure below does not have a vertical line of symmetry, no horizontal?

A) B) C) D)

4.8) How many edges does the figure have?

4.9) How many edges does the figure have?

4.10) How many edges does the figure have?

4.11) How many edges does the figure have?

Croquis of a
Deliberate
Crime

YouTube

4.41) How many edges does the figure have?

4.42) How many edges does the figure have?

4.12) Which of the following figures is made of four congruent shapes

4.13) Given the figure below:

Which figure below appears to be congruent?

4.14) A triangle has three equal sides. If the perimeter is 18 cm how long is each side?

4.15) The following figure was created with two congruent triangle on each end of a rectangle. What is the perimeter of this shape?

4.16) The following figure has a line of symmetry as shown. What is the perimeter of this figure?

4.17) Ed needs to fence his back yard in. The dimensions of the yard are shown below

If he has 103 feet of fence does he have enough to do the job?

For one on one tutoring via skype at $35.00/Hr.; contact me at marksmathtutoring@yahoo.com

4.18) Given the drawings of two rectangles below

What statement below is true
a) The perimeter of A is 40 cm less than the perimeter of B
b) The perimeter of B is 40 cm less than the perimeter of A
c) The perimeter of A is 80 cm less than the perimeter of B
d) The perimeter of B is 80 cm less than the perimeter of A

4.19) The two figures below are drawn with congruent sides.

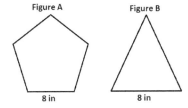

Which statement below is true
a)The perimeter of Figure A is 16 inches larger the Figure B
b)The perimeter of Figure B is 16 inches larger the Figure A
c)The perimeter of Figure A is 24 inches larger the Figure B
d)The perimeter of Figure B and A are the same

4.20) Sarah needs to fence in her garden to keep animals out. The garden has the dimensions shown below

If she has 110 feet of fence, does she have enough?

4.21) Steve has a garden he needs to fence in. He has 64 feet of fence. Which in of the following figure could not be the dimensions of his garden?
a)   c)

b)   d)

4.22) Which of the following figures does not have a perimeter of 120 cm?

a)

c)

b)

d)

4.23) If a triangle has a perimeter of 26 inches, and two sides are 11 inches each. What is the length of the third side?

4.24) What is the area of the letter H below if each square is 1 foot square

4.25) What is the area of the letter L below if each square is 1 foot square

4.26) What is the difference between the area of the letter O and the letter T shown below if each square is I Meter squared

Croquis of a
Deliberate
Crime

YouTube

If you don't get the correct answer, and want an explanation on how to work the problem, go to YouTube and type in "MMT" then the problem number. An example would be, MMT 3.9.w12,. The video will show you how to work problem 3.9.w12.

4.27) Which equation below best describes the mathematical equation to determine the area of the shaded box below?

a) 6-4=2
b) 10X4=40
c) 24÷4=6
d) 6+4=10

4.28) I started to tie my kitchen floor as shown in the diagram below. Each small square is 1 foot square.

Once finished tiling the floor how many ties will be used?

4.29) Given the diagram below what is the area of the rectangle?

4.30) Which of the following rectangles has an area of 42?
a)   c)

b)   d)

4.31) If your floor measures 9 feet by 17 feet, what is the area of this floor in feet square?

 Croquis of a
Deliberate
Crime
YouTube

For one on one tutoring via skype at $35.00/Hr.; contact me at marksmathtutoring@yahoo.com

4.32) If a garden has the shape of the drawing below and each square is 1 meter square, what is the area of the garden?

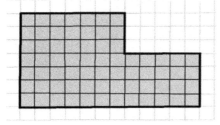

4.33) Which statement below is true about the two figures below

a) The perimeter rectangle A is 56 mm small than rectangle B
b) The perimeter rectangle A is 64 mm small than rectangle B
c) The perimeter rectangle A is 32 mm small than rectangle B

4.53) I a rectangle has sides 45 mm and 20 mm and the smaller side is cut in half, what is its new area?

4.54) If a square has sides 45 inches and is cut to 1/3 what is its new area?

4.55) What is the perimeter of a rectangular poster with one side 18 inches and the other 8 inches.

4.56) If your garden is square with sides 39 feet, what is the perimeter?

4.43) How many smaller blocks are in this cub?

4.44) How many smaller blocks are in this cub?

Croquis of a Deliberate Crime

YouTube

For one on one tutoring via skype at $35.00/Hr.; contact me at marksmathtutoring@yahoo.com

4.45) How many smaller blocks are in this cub?

4.46) How many smaller blocks are in this cub?

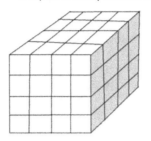

4.47) How many smaller blocks are in this cub?

4.48) How many smaller blocks are in this cub?

4.49) What is the volume of this cube?

2 m

4 m

2 m

4.50) What is the volume of this cube?

6 Ft

10 Ft

4 Ft

4.51) What is the volume of this cube?

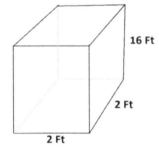

16 Ft

2 Ft

2 Ft

4.52) What is the volume of this cube?

5 m

5 m

5 m

Units

4.34) What would be the best unit of measurement for the size of your dog?
a) Gallons, b) pounds, c) pints, d) Quart

4.35) What would be the best unit of measurement for the distance between you and your school?
a) Gallons, b) miles, c) pints, d) feet

4.36) What would be the best unit of measurement for the amount of milk in your refrigerator?
a) Gallons, b) pounds, c) miles, d) feet

4.37) What would be the best unit of measurement for the distance between you and your TV?
a) Gallons, b) pounds, c) pints, d) feet

Interest
4.38) You parents borrowed $5,000.00 from the bank to buy a car. They repaid $6,500.00. Which statement best explains why they paid the extra $1,500.00
a) They wanted to donate $1,500.00 to the bank to be nice
b) They repaid the loan on a week day and the bank charges money for these days
c) They had extra money and nothing to do with it.
d) The bank charged $1,500.00 in interest for a $6,000.00 loan

4.57) Which of the following is a rotational transformation
a)

b)

c)

d)

4.58) In the drawing below which angle are right angles?

a) <FED, and <EDC
b) <EFA and <FED
c) < CDE and <DCB
d) <FAB and <BCD

4.70) Which two lines in the drawing below appear to be parallel?

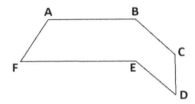

a) AB and BC
b) FE and BC
c) BC and ED
d) CD and AB

4.64) Given the drawing below which two lines appear to be parallel

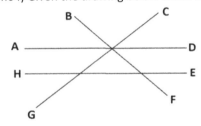

a) Lines BF and CG
b) Lines AD and HE
c) Lines BF and HE
d) Lines AD and BF

4.71) In the figure below which of the following statements is true about the labeled angles

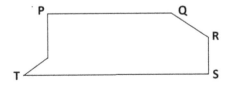

a) 1 right angle, 2 obtuse angles, 2 acute angles
b) 2 right angle, 1 obtuse angles, 2 acute angle
c) 2 right angle, 2 obtuse angles, 1 acute angles
d) 1 right angle, 1 obtuse angles, 3 acute angles

4.72) Which of the following triangle appears to be acute?

4.73) Which of the following triangle appears to be a right angle?

4.74) Which of the following angles appears to be perpendicular?

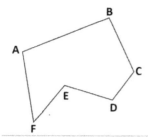

4.75) If I make a triangle with one 90 degrees angle and two acute angles, which statement below describes the figure?
a) Acute triangle
b) Obtuse triangle
c) Right triangle
d) Figure is not a triangle

4.76) If angle <ABC is 41 degrees and angle <CBD is a right angle what is the angle of <ABD

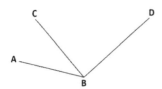

4.77) What is the translation shown in the drawing below?

a) Rotation
b) Translation
c) Reflection
d) none of the above

4.78) Which of the following is not a translation of the following diagram?

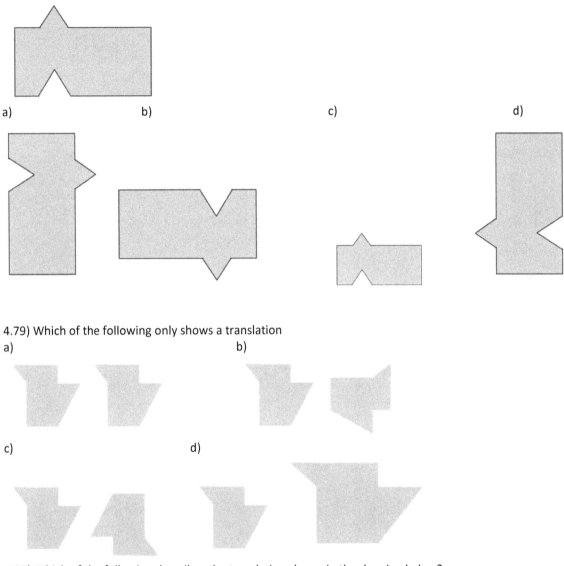

a)   b)   c)   d)

4.79) Which of the following only shows a translation

a)   b)

c)   d)

4.80) Which of the following describes the translation shown in the drawing below?

A) Translation
B) Reflection
c) Rotation
d) no translation

For one on one tutoring via skype at $35.00/Hr.; contact me at marksmathtutoring@yahoo.com

4.81) Which of the following describes the translation shown in the drawing below?

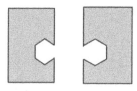

A) Translation
B) Reflection
c) Rotation
d) no translation

4.82) Which of the following describes the translation shown in the drawing below?

A) Translation
B) Reflection
c) Rotation
d) no translation

4.83) Which statement below best describes the three polygons drawn here?

a) All have right angles only
b) All have obtuse only
c) All have acute angles only
d) all of them have parallel lines

4.84) I am going to tile my floor. Part of it is already done and is shaded grey in the diagram below.

What is the area in square feet to be tiled?

For one on one tutoring via skype at $35.00/Hr.; contact me at marksmathtutoring@yahoo.com

4.85) I made a dog kennel. I divided it into three parts as shown in the diagram.

If the area of the small dogs cage is 100 meters square, and the area of the medium dog cage is 250 meters square what is the area of the large dog cage?

4.86) If a square has a side of 15 inches which of the following statements is not true
A) The perimeter is 60 inches
B) The length of the other sides are 15 inches
C) The area of the square is 225 inches square
D) We don't know the length of the other sides

Croquis of a
Deliberate
Crime

YouTube

If you don't get the correct answer, and want an explanation on how to work the problem, go to YouTube and type in "MMT" then the problem number. An example would be, MMT 3.9.w12,. The video will show you how to work problem 3.9.w12.

For one on one tutoring via skype at $35.00/Hr.; contact me at marksmathtutoring@yahoo.com

5.0 FRACTIONS

A)   B)   C)   D)   E)

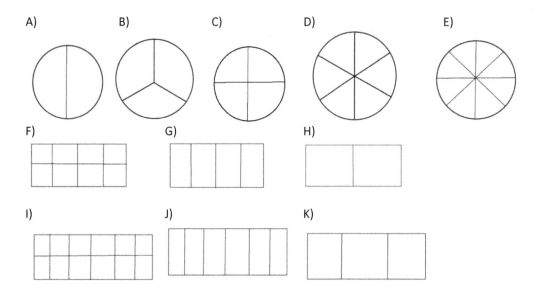

F)   G)   H)

I)   J)   K)

For the following problems redraw each figure before shading in the parts. This way you can reuse them.
5.1) for figure A) color ½ of the circle
5.2) for figure B) color 2/3 of the circle
5.3) for figure I) color 7/12 of the square
5.4) for figure J) color 5/6 of the square
5.5) for figure F) color 5/8 of the square
5.6) for figure E) color 5/8 of the circle

5.7) color 2/4 of figure C) and 1/2 of Figure A) Are they the same?
5.8) color 3/4 of figure C) and 6/8 of Figure E) Are they the same?
5.9) color 2/3 of figure B) and 3/6 of Figure D) Are they the same?
5.10) color 2/8 of figure E) and 1/4 of Figure C) Are they the same?
5.11) color 2/4 of figure G) and 2/8 of Figure F) Are they the same?
5.12) color 6/12 of figure I) and 3/4 of Figure G) Are they the same?
5.13) color 2/3 of figure K) and 4/6 of Figure J) Are they the same?

5.14) color 2/4 of figure C) and 3/8 of Figure E) Are they the same? If not which one is greater?
5.15) color 2/3 of figure B) and 3/6 of Figure D) Are they the same? If not which one is less?
5.16) color 3/8 of figure E) and 3/4 of Figure C) Are they the same? If not which one is less?
5.17) color 1/3 of figure B) and 3/8 of Figure E) Are they the same? If not which one is greater?
5.18) color 3/4 of figure G) and 1/2 of Figure H) Are they the same? If not which one is greater?
5.19) color 1/3 of figure K) and 1/3 of Figure J) Are they the same? If not which one is less?
5.20) color 4/12 of figure I) and 1/3 of Figure K) Are they the same? If not which one is greater?
5.21) color 2/12 of figure I) and 2/6 of Figure J) Are they the same? If not which one is greater?
5.22) color 2/6 of figure J) and 2/3 of Figure K) Are they the same? If not which one is greater?
5.23) color 2/4 of figure G) and 4/8 of Figure F) Are they the same? If not which one is greater?
5.24) color 4/6 of figure J) and 1/2 of Figure H) Are they the same? If not which one is less?
5.25) color 6/12 of figure I) and 3/6 of Figure J) Are they the same? If not which one is less?
5.27) color 2/12 of figure I) and 2/6 of Figure J) Are they the same? If not which one is greater?
5.28) color 1/3 of figure K) and 2/6 of Figure J) Are they the same? If not which one is less?
5.29) color 1/8 of figure F) and 1/4 of Figure G) Are they the same? If not which one is greater?

5.30) Sarah shaded the following figure

Which fraction best represtents the shaded area
a) 2/3, b) 3/4, c) 1/2, d) 4/4

5.31) Edward shaded the following figure

Which fraction best represents the shaded area
a) 1/4, b) 3/2, c) 2/3, d) 1/3

5.32) Mike saded th following figure

Which fraction best represents the saded area
a) 1/8, b) 1/4, c) 1/2, d) 7/8

5.33) Jonny shaded the following figure

Which fraction best represents the saded area
a) 5/8, b) 8/12, c) 2/3, d) 3/4

5.34) Lynne saded the following figure

Which fraction best represents the shaded area
a) 4/6, b) 3/4, c) 2/3, d) 3/5

5.35) Lynne saded the following figure

Which fraction best represents the shaded area
a) 7/8, b) 1/8, c) 3/4, d) 5/8

5.36) Sarah ate 1/3 of a cake and her brother ate 1/4 of a pie. Which one ate the most cake?
5.37) If one apple is 3/4 of a pound and the other is 3/5 of a pound. Which apple is bigger?
5.38) If I buy 2/5 of a pound of sugar and you buy 2/3 of a pound of sugar, who bought the most?
5.39) If Al pays 3/4 of a dollar and Sue pays 3/5 of a dollar who pays the most?
5.40) Which number is smaller 1/2 or 1/3?
5.41) Which number is larger 2/3 or 2/5?
5.42) which number is larger 3/5 or 3/8?
5.43) Which number is smaller 5/8 or 5/9

5.44) Which fraction is larger 2/5 or 3/5?
5.45) which fraction is larger 1/3 or 2/3?
5.46) Which fraction is smaller 3/8 or 6/8?
5.47) which fraction is smaller 5/6 or 3/6?

Croquis of a
Deliberate
Crime

YouTube

If you don't get the correct answer, and want an explanation on how to work the problem, go to YouTube and type in "MMT" then the problem number. An example would be, MMT 3.9.w12,. The video will show you how to work problem 3.9.w12.

5.48) Verna shaded the following two figures

Which statements best describes the shaded areas
a) 7/8<5/8
b) 3/4>5/8
c)3/4>7/8
d) 7/8>5/8

5.50) the following shapes are shaded as shown.

Which stament below best describes this shading
a)5/6>4/6, b) 2/6>3/6, c) 3/4< 2/3, d) 5/6=4/6

5.52) the following shapes are shaded as shown.

Which stament below best describes this shading
a)3/8>6/8, b) 3/8<6/8, c) 2/4< 2/8, d) 5/6<4/6

5.49) Verna shaded the following two figures

Which statements best describes the shaded areas
a) 3/4>1/4
b) 1/4>3/4
c) 1/2<1/4
d) 1/4<3/4

5.51) the following shapes are shaded as shown.

Which stament below best describes this shading
a)5/6>4/6, b) 3/8>3/6, c) 10/12< 3/12, d)10/12>3/12

5.53) the following shapes are shaded as shown.

Which stament below best describes this shading
a)2/3>1/3, b) 2/3<1/3, c) 1/4>2/6, d) 4/6<2/6

5.54) Which statement is true
    a) 1/8<1/5<1/4<1/3, b) 1/3<1/4<1/6<1/9, c) 2/5<2/4<2/6<2/8, d) 3/5>3/7>3/8>3/2
5.55) Which statement is true
    a) 3/5<3/4<3/2<3/7, b) 3/4>3/5>3/7>3/8, c) 4/5<4/6<4/7<4/9, d) 4/5>4/6>4/3>4/8
5.56) Which statement is true
    a) 5/7>5/8>5/4>5/6, b) 4/5>4/6>4/7>4/9, c) 3/5<3/4<3/7<3/9 d) 6/7<6/4<6/5<6/9
5.57) Which statement is true
    a) 2/3<3/3<4/3<5/3, b) 3/9>5/9>6/9<1/9, c) 6/7>5/7>7/7>3/7, d) 5/6>5/4>5/3>5/2
5.58) Which statement is true
    a) 5/8<7/8<3/8<6/8, b) 3/7<9/7<6/7<8/7, c) 7/8>6/8>5/8>3/8, d) 12/4<3/4<6/4<3/4

5.59) The diagram below show the amount of money I found in the street today.

How much money is this
a) 1\frac{51}{}$
b) 1\frac{96}{}$
c) 1\frac{47}{}$
d) 1\frac{37}{}$

5.60) I want to buy a candy bar. It cost $1^{86}. If the diagram below shows how much money I have in my pocket do I have enough money?

($1) ($1) (25¢) (10¢) (10¢) (10¢) (5¢) (5¢) (1¢) (1¢)

5.61) Is the amount of money shown below more than $0^{87}?

(25¢) (25¢) (10¢) (10¢) (5¢) (5¢) (5¢) (1¢) (1¢)

5.62) The drawing below shows four different amounts of money. Which one has a 7 in the tenths place?

a)

($5) ($5) (25¢) (25¢)
($1) ($1) (25¢) (10¢) (5¢) (1¢)

b)

($1) ($1) (25¢)
($1) ($1) (10¢) (10¢) (5¢) (5¢) (1¢) (1¢) (1¢)

c)

($5) ($5) (25¢) (10¢) (10¢) (5¢) (5¢) (5¢) (1¢)

d)

($1) ($1) (25¢) (25¢) (10¢) (5¢) (5¢) (1¢) (1¢) (1¢)

5.63) The drawing below represents which relationship?

a) 7>3
b) $^7/_{10}$>$^3/_5$
c) 3>2
d) $^3/_{10}$>$^2/_5$

Croquis of a
Deliberate
Crime

YouTube

5.64) Given the diagram below

1					
1/2			1/2		
1/3		1/3		1/3	
1/4	1/4		1/4		1/4
1/5	1/5	1/5	1/5		1/5
1/6	1/6	1/6	1/6	1/6	1/6

Which of the following statements is true
a) 1/6>1/5>1/4>1/3
b) 2/6< 2/5< 1/4< 2/3
c) 4/6>3/5>2/4>1/3
d) 1/2>2/3>3/4>4/5

5.65) Given the following statements which one is greater than $0.93.

Fraction Addition

5.2.1) 1/2+1/2	5.2.2) 2/3+3/3	5.2.3) 5/6+1/6	5.2.4) 3/4+2/4
5.2.5) 5/8+2/8	5.2.6) 6/9+4/9	5.2.7) 1/5+3/5	5.2.8) 2/6+4/6
5.2.9) 3/9+ 2/9	5.2.10) 4/7+2/7	5.2.11) 1/3+1/3	5.2.12) 4/6+1/6
5.2.13) 3/8+2/8	5.2.14) 4/7+1/7	5.2.15) 2/11+6/11	5.2.16) 5/16+4/16
5.2.17) 2/8+4/8	5.2.18) 3/7+2/7	5.2.19) 6/12+5/12	5.2.20) 5/13+7/13
5.2.21) 4/12+6/12	5.2.22) 4/15+8/15	5.2.23) 6/11+3/11	5.2.24) 7/10+4/10

5.2.25)3/4+1/3	5.2.26)2/3+1/6	5.2.27)3/4+4/5	5.2.28)2/7+1/2
5.2.29)5/7+2/3	5.2.30)2/3+2/7	5.2.31)3/7+5/6	5.2.32)3/5+1/2
5.2.33)2/5+1/4	5.2.34)3/7+7/8	5.2.35)3/7+3/5	5.2.36)2/7+1/4
5.2.37)5/7+1/5	5.2.38)1/8+1/3	5.2.39)2/7+1/3	5.2.40)1/6+3/8
5.2.41)3/7+1/3	5.2.42)3/7+2/3	5.2.43)6/7+5/8	5.2.44)6/7+3/4
5.2.45)1/3+5/6	5.2.46)1/3+1/2	5.2.47)2/5+1/6	5.2.48)3/4+5/6
5.2.49)1/6+1/3	5.2.50)1/4+1/6	5.2.51)2/5+5/6	5.2.52)3/7+4/5
5.2.53)2/3+1/5	5.2.54)3/4+2/3	5.2.55)1/3+5/7	5.2.56)5/8+5/6

5.2.57)$1\,^2/_3+2\,^1/_4$	5.2.58)$2\,^1/_6+2\,^3/_4$	5.2.59)$3\,^1/_5+1\,^1/_4$	5.2.60)$2\,^1/_8+1\,^1/_7$
	5.2.61)$2\,^5/_8+1\,^1/_3$	5.2.62)$1\,^5/_7+3\,^5/_6$	5.2.63)$2\,^2/_7+3\,^1/_2$
5.2.64)$1\,^3/_5+2\,^3/_8$	5.2.65)$1\,^3/_5+2\,^6/_7$	5.2.66)$1\,^1/_4+1\,^1/_3$	5.2.67)$1\,^1/_3+3\,^1/_5$
5.2.68)$1\,^2/_7+4\,^1/_5$	5.2.69)$1\,^4/_7+3\,^2/_3$	5.2.70)$1\,^5/_8+2\,^4/_7$	5.2.71)$2\,^1/_4+2\,^5/_6$
5.2.72)$2\,^1/_2+3\,^5/_7$	5.2.73)$3\,^1/_7+2\,^1/_6$	5.2.74)$1\,^3/_8+4\,^2/_3$	5.2.75)$1\,^1/_6+2\,^1/_5$

5.2.76) $2\,^4/_7+2\,^2/_5$ 5.2.77) $1\,^2/_5+1\,^1/_6$ 5.2.78) $2\,^7/_8+2\,^1/_6$ 5.2.79) $1\,^2/_5+3\,^7/_8$

5.2.80) $1\,^2/_7+4\,^1/_5$ 5.2.81) $1\,^4/_7+3\,^2/_3$ 5.2.82) $1\,^5/_8+2\,^4/_7$ 5.2.83) $2\,^1/_4+2\,^5/_8$

5.2.84) $2\,^5/_8+3\,^4/_5$ 5.2.85) $2\,^1/_4+2\,^4/_5$ 5.2.86) $1\,^4/_5+3\,^6/_7$ 5.2.87) $1\,^3/_8+2\,^3/_7$

5.2.88) $3+2^3/_7$ 5.2.89) $1+6^5/_8$ 5.2.90) $5+8^7/_8$ 5.2.91) $8+3^1/_6$

5.2.92) $9+2^5/_8$ 5.2.93) $9^8/_9+4$ 5.2.94) $3+1^2/_9$ 5.2.95) $5^3/_7+4$

5.2.96) $4+2^3/_5$ 5.2.97) $2^4/_7+6$ 5.2.98) $1+8^2/_9$ 5.2.99) $2^4/_9+7$

5.2.100) (2/3)+(-1/4)   5.2.101) (-2/5)+(-1/3)   5.2.102) (1/5)+(-1/4)   5.2.103) (-1/8)+(1/4)

5.2.104) (-5/6)+(1/3)   5.2.105) (-4/7)+(-2/3)   5.2.106) (2/5)+(-5/7)   5.2.107) (-1/2)+(-4/5)

5.2.108) (-3/4)+(2/3)   5.2.109) (6/8)+(-2/3)   5.2.110) (-3/5)+(-5/6)   5.2.111) (-1/2)+(2/6)

5.2.112) $(1^2/_3)+(-1^3/_4)$ 5.2.113) $(-2\,^4/_5)+(-1^1/_3)$ 5.2.114) $(-2\,^1/_3)+(^5/_6)$ 5.2.115) $(3\,^1/_3)+(-1\,^4/_5)$

5.2.116) $(-2\,^1/_3)+(-2\,\frac{1}{2})$ 5.2.117) $(-3\,\frac{1}{4})+(-2/3)$ 5.2.118) $(-1\,^2/_3)+(-1\,^3/_5)$ 5.2.119) $(-1^3/_4)+(2\,^1/_3)$

5.2.120) $(-2\,\frac{1}{4})+(-2\,^3/_5)$ 5.2.121) $(-1\,^6/_8)+(2\,\frac{1}{2})$ 5.2.122) $(-3\,^2/_3)+(-1\,^3/_5)$ 5.2.123) $(2\,\frac{1}{2})+(-3\,\frac{1}{4})$

5.2.124) $(2)+(-1^3/_4)$ 5.2.125) $(-3)+(-1^1/_3)$ 5.2.126) $(-1)+(^5/_6)$ 5.2.127) $(2)+(-1\,^4/_5)$

5.2.128) $(-2\,^1/_3)+(-1)$ 5.2.129) $(-3\,\frac{1}{4})+(-2)$ 5.2.130) $(-1\,^2/_3)+(-1)$ 5.2.131) $(-1^3/_4)+(2)$

5.2.w1) If I share a cake with a friend in the proportions shown below.

Me   my friend

What fraction best describes the amount of cake eaten?

a) 11/12   b) 8/12   c) 2/3   d) ¾

5.2.w2) If I have 2/3 of a pound and you have 3/4 of a pond how much do we have combined

5.2.w3) If I walk 5/6 of a mile before lunch and 3/5 of a mile after lunch how far did I walk

5.2.w4) If my fish weights 4/5 of a pound and my friends weights 2/3 of a pound how much do they weight together

5.2.w5) If I have 5/6 a dollar and borrow another 2/5 of a dollar how much do I have

5.2.w6) If one piece of paper is 7/8 foot long and the other is 2/3 foot long how long are they combined

5.2.w7) My dog eat 5/6 pound of food and yours eats 2/3 pound how much did they eat combined

5.2.w8) If I have ¾ pound of grapes and you have $2\,^2/_3$ pound of grapes how much do we have combined

5.2.w9) If I have $4\,^5/_6$ dollar in my pocket and 2 ¾ in my piggy bank how much do I have total

5.2.w10) My fish weights $12\,^4/_5$ pound and another guys weights 5 ¾ how much do they weight combined

5.2.w11) I have 3 feet of rope and you have 1 ¾ foot piece how long are they combined

For one on one tutoring via skype at $35.00/Hr.; contact me at marksmathtutoring@yahoo.com

Fraction Subtraction

5.3.1) 1/2-1/2	5.3.2) 2/3-1/3	5.3.3) 5/6-1/6	5.3.4) 3/4-1/4
5.3.5) 5/8-3/8	5.3.6) 6/9-4/9	5.3.7) 4/5-3/5	5.3.8) 5/6-4/6
5.3.9) 3/9- 2/9	5.3.10) 4/7-2/7	5.3.11) 1/3-1/3	5.3.12) 4/6-1/6
5.3.13) 3/8-2/8	5.3.14) 4/7-1/7	5.3.15) 2/11-1/11	5.3.16) 5/16-4/16
5.3.17) 12/8-4/8	5.3.18) 3/7-2/7	5.3.19) 6/12-5/12	5.3.20) 5/13-2/13
5.3.21) 7/12-6/12	5.3.22) 8/15-5/15	5.3.23) 6/11-3/11	5.3.24) 7/10-4/10

5.3.25)3/4-1/3	5.3.26)2/3-1/6	5.3.27)3/4-4/5	5.3.28)2/7-1/2
5.3.29)5/7-2/3	5.3.30)2/3-2/7	5.3.31)3/7-5/6	5.3.32)3/5-1/2
5.3.33)2/5-1/4	5.3.34)3/7-7/8	5.3.35)3/7-3/5	5.3.36)2/7-1/4
5.3.37)5/7-1/5	5.3.38)1/8-1/3	5.3.39)1/8-1/9	5.3.40)1/6-3/8
5.3.41)3/7-1/3	5.3.42)3/7-2/3	5.3.43)6/7-5/8	5.3.44)6/7-3/4
5.3.45)1/3-5/6	5.3.46)1/3-1/2	5.3.47)2/5-1/6	5.3.48)3/4-5/6
5.3.49)1/6-1/3	5.3.50)1/4-1/6	5.3.51)2/5-5/6	5.3.52)3/7-4/5
5.3.53)2/3-1/5	5.3.54)3/4-2/3	5.3.55)1/3-5/7	5.3.56)5/8-5/6

5.3.57)$1\,^2/_3$-$2\,^1/_4$	5.3.58)$2\,^1/_6$-$2\,^3/_4$	5.3.59)$3\,^1/_5$-$1\,^1/_4$	5.3.60)$2\,^1/_8$-$1\,^1/_7$
5.3.60)$2\,^5/_8$-$3\,^2/_5$	5.3.61)$2\,^5/_8$-$1\,^1/_3$	5.3.62)$1\,^5/_7$-$3\,^5/_6$	5.3.63)$2\,^2/_7$-$3\,^1/_2$
5.3.64)$1\,^3/_5$-$2\,^3/_8$	5.3.65)$1\,^3/_5$-$2\,^6/_7$	5.3.66)$1\,^1/_4$-$1\,^1/_3$	5.3.67)$1\,^1/_3$-$3\,^1/_5$
5.3.68)$1\,^2/_7$-$4\,^1/_5$	5.3.69)$1\,^4/_7$-$3\,^2/_3$	5.3.70)$1\,^5/_8$-$2\,^4/_7$	5.3.71)$2\,^1/_4$-$2\,^5/_6$
5.3.72)$2\,^1/_2$-$3\,^5/_7$	5.3.73)$3\,^1/_7$-$2\,^1/_6$	5.3.74)$1\,^3/_8$-$4\,^2/_3$	5.3.75)$1\,^1/_6$-$2\,^1/_5$
5.3.76)$2\,^4/_7$-$2\,^2/_5$	5.3.77)$1\,^2/_5$-$1\,^1/_6$	5.3.78)$2\,^7/_8$-$2\,^1/_6$	5.3.79)$1\,^2/_5$-$3\,^7/_8$
5.3.80)$1\,^2/_7$-$4\,^1/_5$	5.3.81)$1\,^4/_7$-$3\,^2/_3$	5.3.82)$1\,^5/_8$-$2\,^4/_7$	5.3.83)$2\,^1/_4$-$2\,^5/_8$
5.3.84)$2\,^5/_8$-$3\,^4/_5$	5.3.85)$2\,^1/_4$-$2\,^4/_5$	5.3.86)$1\,^4/_5$-$3\,^6/_7$	5.3.87)$1\,^3/_8$-$2\,^3/_7$
5.3.88) 3-$2\,^3/_7$	5.3.89) 1-$6\,^5/_8$	5.3.90) 5-$8\,^7/_8$	5.3.91) 8-$3\,^1/_6$
5.3.92) 9-$2\,^5/_8$	5.3.93) $9\,^8/_9$-4	5.3.94)3-$1\,^2/_9$	5.3.95)$5\,^3/_7$-4
5.3.96) 4-$2\,^3/_5$	5.3.97) $2\,^4/_7$-6	5.3.98) 1-$8\,^2/_9$	5.3.99)$2\,^4/_9$-7

5.3.100) 2/3-(-1/4)	5.3.101) (-2/5)-(-1/3)	5.3.102) (1/5)-(-1/4)	5.3.103) (-1/8)-(1/4)
5.3.104) (-5/6)-(1/3)	5.3.105) (-4/7)-(-2/3)	5.3.106) (2/5)-(-5/7)	5.3.107) (-1/2)-(-4/5)
5.3.108) (-3/4)-(2/3)	5.3.109) (6/8)-(-2/3)	5.3.110) (-3/5)-(-5/6)	5.3.111) (-1/2)-(2/6)

5.3.112) $(1\,^2/_3)$-$(-1\,^3/_4)$	5.3.113) $(-2\,^4/_5)$-$(-1\,^1/_3)$	5.3.114) $(-2\,^1/_3)$-$(^5/_6)$	5.3.115) $(3\,^1/_3)$-$(-1\,^4/_5)$
5.3.116) $(-2\,^1/_3)$-(-2 ½)	5.3.117) (-3 ¼)-(-2/3)	5.3.118) $(-1\,^2/_3)$-$(-1\,^3/_5)$	5.3.119) $(-1\,^3/_4)$-$(2\,^1/_3)$
5.3.120) (-2 ¼)-$(-2\,^3/_5)$	5.3.121) $(-1\,^6/_8)$-(2 ½)	5.3.122) $(-3\,^2/_3)$-$(-1\,^3/_5)$	5.3.123) (2 ½)-(-3 ¼)

5.3.124) (2)-$(-1\,^3/_4)$	5.3.125) (-3)-$(-1\,^1/_3)$	5.3.126) (-1)-$(^5/_6)$	5.3.127) (2)-$(-1\,^4/_5)$
5.3.128) $(-2\,^1/_3)$-(-1)	5.3.129) (-3 ¼)-(-2)	5.3.130) $(-1\,^2/_3)$-(-1)	5.3.131) $(-1\,^3/_4)$-(2)

5.3.w1) If I cut pieces of paper into two shapes shown below

⃝⃝◠⃝⃝
◠◠⃝◠

What is the best way to determine the fractional differences between these two shapes?
a)10/10-6/10=
b)10/10-4/10=
c)6/10-4/10=
d)6/10+4/10=

5.3.w2) I am 6 ½ away from a fountain. My dog is 4 1/3 feet closer to the fountain. What is the distance between me and my dog.

5.3.w4) given the diagram below

Which statement below best represents the difference shown?
a) 9/12-4/12
b)12/12-9/12
c) 12/12-4/12
d) 9/12+4/12

5.3.w5) If I have $^4/_5$ dollar and buy a burger for ¾ dollar how much do I have left over

5.3.w6) If I my mom sends me to the store for 3/5 pound of grapes but they only have 1/2 pound how much more do I need

5.3.w7) If I am making cookies and they require ¾ pound of butter and I have 7/9 pound how much will I have left over

5.3.w8) If I have a rope that is 8/9 foot long and I cut ½ foot out of it how long in her piece left over

5.3.w9) If I need 3/5 of a dollar to buy a candy bar and have 8/9 of a dollar how much change will I have left over

5.3.w10) What is the difference between the weight of my fish and my friends if mine weights $3\,^6/_7$ and his weights $2\,^4/_5$

5.3.w11) If I have $4\,^4/_5$ dollar and buy a burger for 2 ¾ dollar how much do I have left over

5.3.w12) If I have a rope 5 3/5 foot long and cut a piece 2 4/5 out of it how much rope do I have left

Fraction Multiplication

5.4.1) 1/2X1/2	5.4.2) 2/3X1/3	5.4.3) 5/6X1/6	5.4.4) 3/4X1/4
5.4.5) 5/8X3/8	5.4.6) 6/9X4/9	5.4.7) 4/5X3/5	5.4.8) 5/6X4/6

5.4.9)3/4X1/3	5.4.10)2/3X1/6	5.4.11)3/4X4/5	5.4.12)2/7X1/2
5.4.13)5/7X2/3	5.4.14)2/3X2/7	5.4.15)3/7X5/6	5.4.16)3/5X1/2
5.4.17)2/5X1/4	5.4.18)3/7X7/8	5.4.19)3/7X3/5	5.4.20)2/7X1/4
5.4.21)5/7X1/5	5.4.22)1/8X1/3	5.4.23)3/8X2/3	5.4.24)1/6X3/8
5.4.25)3/7X1/3	5.4.26)3/7X2/3	5.4.27)6/7X5/8	5.4.28)6/7X3/4
5.4.29)1/3X5/6	5.4.30)1/3X1/2	5.4.31)2/5X1/6	5.4.32)3/4X5/6
5.4.33)1/6X1/3	5.4.34)1/4X1/6	5.4.35)2/5X5/6	5.4.36)3/7X4/5
5.4.37)2/3X1/5	5.4.38)3/4X2/3	5.4.39)1/3X5/7	5.4.40)5/8X5/6

5.4.41)$1\,^2/_3$X$2\,^1/_4$	5.4.42)$2\,^1/_6$X$2\,^3/_4$	5.4.43)$3\,^1/_5$X$1\,^1/_4$	5.4.44)$2\,^1/_8$X$1\,^1/_7$
5.4.45)$2\,^5/_8$X$3\,^2/_5$	5.4.46)$2\,^5/_8$X$1\,^1/_3$	5.4.47)$1\,^5/_7$X$3\,^5/_6$	5.4.48)$2\,^2/_7$X$3\,^1/_2$
5.4.49)$1\,^3/_5$X$2\,^3/_8$	5.4.50) $1\,^3/_5$X$2\,^6/_7$	5.4.51) $1\,^1/_4$X$1\,^1/_3$	5.4.52)$1\,^1/_3$X$3\,^1/_5$
5.4.53)$1\,^2/_7$X$4\,^1/_5$	5.4.54) $1\,^4/_7$X$3\,^2/_3$	5.4.55) $1\,^5/_8$X$2\,^4/_7$	5.4.56)$2\,^1/_4$X$2\,^5/_6$
5.4.57)$2\,^1/_2$X$3\,^5/_7$	5.4.58) $3\,^1/_7$X$2\,^1/_6$	5.4.59) $1\,^3/_8$X$4\,^2/_3$	5.4.60)$1\,^1/_6$X$2\,^1/_5$
5.4.61)$2\,^4/_7$X$2\,^2/_5$	5.4.62)$1\,^2/_5$X$1\,^1/_6$	5.4.63)$2\,^7/_8$X$2\,^1/_6$	5.4.64)$1\,^2/_5$X$3\,^7/_8$
5.4.65)$1\,^2/_7$X$4\,^1/_5$	5.4.66)$1\,^4/_7$X$3\,^2/_3$	5.4.67)$1\,^5/_8$X$2\,^4/_7$	5.4.68)$2\,^1/_4$X$2\,^5/_8$
5.4.69)$2\,^5/_8$X$3\,^4/_5$	5.4.70)$2\,^1/_4$X$2\,^4/_5$	5.4.71)$1\,^4/_5$X$3\,^6/_7$	5.4.72)$1\,^3/_8$X$2\,^3/_7$

5.4.73) $3X2\frac{3}{7}$ 5.4.74) $1X6\frac{5}{8}$ 5.4.75) $5X8\frac{7}{8}$ 5.4.76) $8X3\frac{1}{6}$

5.4.77) $9X2\frac{5}{8}$ 5.4.78) $9\frac{8}{9}X4$ 5.4.79) $3X1\frac{2}{9}$ 5.4.80) $5\frac{3}{7}X4$

5.4.81) $4X2\frac{3}{5}$ 5.4.82) $2\frac{4}{7}X6$ 5.4.83) $1X8\frac{2}{9}$ 5.4.84) $2\frac{4}{9}X7$

5.4.100) $2/3x(-1/4)$ 5.4.101) $(-2/5)x(-1/3)$ 5.4.102) $(1/5)x(-1/4)$ 5.4.103) $(-1/8)x(1/4)$

5.4.104) $(-5/6)x(1/3)$ 5.4.105) $(-4/7)x(-2/3)$ 5.4.106) $(2/5)x(-5/7)$ 5.4.107) $(-1/2)x(-4/5)$

5.4.108) $(-3/4)x(2/3)$ 5.4.109) $(6/8)x(-2/3)$ 5.4.110) $(-3/5)x(-5/6)$ 5.4.111) $(-1/2)x(2/6)$

5.4.112) $(1\frac{2}{3})x(-1\frac{3}{4})$ 5.4.113) $(-2\frac{4}{5})x(-1\frac{1}{3})$ 5.4.114) $(-2\frac{1}{3})x(\frac{5}{6})$ 5.4.115) $(3\frac{1}{3})x(-1\frac{4}{5})$

5.4.116) $(-2\frac{1}{3})x(-2\frac{1}{2})$ 5.4.117) $(-3\frac{1}{4})x(-2/3)$ 5.4.118) $(-1\frac{2}{3})x(-1\frac{3}{5})$ 5.4.119) $(-1\frac{3}{4})x(2\frac{1}{3})$

5.4.120) $(-2\frac{1}{4})x(-2\frac{3}{5})$ 5.4.121) $(-1\frac{6}{8})x(2\frac{1}{2})$ 5.4.122) $(-3\frac{2}{3})x(-1\frac{3}{5})$ 5.4.123) $(2\frac{1}{2})x(-3\frac{1}{4})$

5.4.124) $(2)x(-1\frac{3}{4})$ 5.4.125) $(-3)x(-1\frac{1}{3})$ 5.4.126) $(-1)x(\frac{5}{6})$ 5.4.127) $(2)x(-1\frac{4}{5})$

5.4.128) $(-2\frac{1}{3})x(-1)$ 5.4.129) $(-3\frac{1}{4})x(-2)$ 5.4.130) $(-1\frac{2}{3})x(-1)$ 5.4.131) $(-1\frac{3}{4})x(2)$

Fraction Division

5.5.1) $1/2\div1/2$ 5.5.2) $2/3\div1/3$ 5.5.3) $5/6\div1/6$ 5.5.4) $3/4\div1/4$

5.5.5) $5/8\div3/8$ 5.5.6) $6/9\div4/9$ 5.5.7) $4/5\div3/5$ 5.5.8) $5/6\div4/6$

5.5.9) $3/4\div1/3$ 5.5.10) $2/3\div1/6$ 5.5.11) $3/4\div4/5$ 5.5.12) $2/7\div1/2$

5.5.13) $5/7\div2/3$ 5.5.14) $2/3\div2/7$ 5.5.15) $3/7\div5/6$ 5.5.16) $3/5\div1/2$

5.5.17) $2/5\div1/4$ 5.5.18) $3/7\div7/8$ 5.5.19) $3/7\div3/5$ 5.5.20) $2/7\div1/4$

5.5.21) $5/7\div1/5$ 5.5.22) $1/8\div1/3$ 5.5.23) $1/9\div1/2$ 5.5.24) $1/6\div3/8$

5.5.25) $3/7\div1/3$ 5.5.26) $3/7\div2/3$ 5.5.27) $6/7\div5/8$ 5.5.28) $6/7\div3/4$

5.5.29) $1/3\div5/6$ 5.5.30) $1/3\div1/2$ 5.5.31) $2/5\div1/6$ 5.5.32) $3/4\div5/6$

5.5.33) $1/6\div1/3$ 5.5.34) $1/4\div1/6$ 5.5.35) $2/5\div5/6$ 5.5.36) $3/7\div4/5$

5.5.37) $2/3\div1/5$ 5.5.38) $3/4\div2/3$ 5.5.39) $1/3\div5/7$ 5.5.40) $5/8\div5/6$

5.5.41) $1\frac{2}{3}\div2\frac{1}{4}$ 5.5.42) $2\frac{1}{6}\div2\frac{3}{4}$ 5.5.43) $3\frac{1}{5}\div1\frac{1}{4}$ 5.5.44) $2\frac{1}{8}\div1\frac{1}{7}$

5.5.45) $2\frac{5}{8}\div3\frac{2}{5}$ 5.5.46) $2\frac{5}{8}\div1\frac{1}{3}$ 5.5.47) $1\frac{5}{7}\div3\frac{5}{6}$ 5.5.48) $2\frac{2}{7}\div3\frac{1}{2}$

5.5.49) $1\frac{3}{5}\div2\frac{3}{8}$ 5.5.50) $1\frac{3}{5}\div2\frac{6}{7}$ 5.5.51) $1\frac{1}{4}\div1\frac{1}{3}$ 5.5.52) $1\frac{1}{3}\div3\frac{1}{5}$

5.5.53) $1\frac{1}{7}\div4\frac{1}{5}$ 5.5.54) $1\frac{4}{7}\div3\frac{2}{3}$ 5.5.55) $1\frac{5}{8}\div2\frac{4}{7}$ 5.5.56) $2\frac{1}{4}\div2\frac{5}{6}$

5.5.57) $2\frac{1}{2}\div3\frac{5}{7}$ 5.5.58) $3\frac{1}{7}\div2\frac{1}{6}$ 5.5.59) $1\frac{3}{8}\div4\frac{2}{3}$ 5.5.60) $1\frac{1}{6}\div2\frac{1}{5}$

5.5.61) $2\frac{4}{7}\div2\frac{2}{5}$ 5.5.62) $1\frac{2}{5}\div1\frac{1}{6}$ 5.5.63) $2\frac{7}{8}\div2\frac{1}{6}$ 5.5.64) $1\frac{2}{5}\div3\frac{7}{8}$

5.5.65) $1\frac{2}{7}\div4\frac{1}{5}$ 5.5.66) $1\frac{4}{7}\div3\frac{2}{3}$ 5.5.67) $1\frac{5}{8}\div2\frac{4}{7}$ 5.5.68) $2\frac{1}{4}\div2\frac{5}{8}$

5.5.69) $2\frac{5}{8}\div3\frac{4}{5}$ 5.5.70) $2\frac{1}{4}\div2\frac{4}{5}$ 5.5.71) $1\frac{4}{5}\div3\frac{6}{7}$ 5.5.72) $1\frac{3}{8}\div2\frac{3}{7}$

5.5.73) $3\div2\frac{3}{7}$ 5.5.74) $1\div6\frac{5}{8}$ 5.5.75) $5\div8\frac{7}{8}$ 5.5.76) $8\div3\frac{1}{6}$

5.5.77) $9\div2\frac{5}{8}$ 5.5.78) $9\frac{8}{9}\div4$ 5.5.79) $3\div1\frac{2}{9}$ 5.5.80) $5\frac{3}{7}\div4$

5.5.81) $4\div2\frac{3}{5}$ 5.5.82) $2\frac{4}{7}\div6$ 5.5.83) $1\div8\frac{2}{9}$ 5.5.84) $2\frac{4}{9}\div7$

5.5.100) $2/3\div(-1/4)$ 5.5.101) $(-2/5)\div(-1/3)$ 5.5.102) $(1/5)\div(-1/4)$ 5.5.103) $(-1/8)\div(1/4)$

5.5.104) $(-5/6)\div(1/3)$ 5.5.105) $(-4/7)\div(-2/3)$ 5.5.106) $(2/5)\div(-5/7)$ 5.5.107) $(-1/2)\div(-4/5)$

5.5.108) $(-3/4)\div(2/3)$ 5.5.109) $(6/8)\div(-2/3)$ 5.5.110) $(-3/5)\div(-5/6)$ 5.5.111) $(-1/2)\div(2/6)$

5.5.112) $(1\frac{2}{3})\div(-1\frac{3}{4})$ 5.5.113) $(-2\frac{4}{5})\div(-1\frac{1}{3})$ 5.5.114) $(-2\frac{1}{3})\div(\frac{5}{6})$ 5.5.115) $(3\frac{1}{3})\div(-1\frac{4}{5})$

5.5.116) $(-2\frac{1}{3})\div(-2\frac{1}{2})$ 5.5.117) $(-3\frac{1}{4})\div(-2/3)$ 5.5.118) $(-1\frac{2}{3})\div(-1\frac{3}{5})$ 5.5.119) $(-1\frac{3}{4})\div(2\frac{1}{3})$

5.5.120) $(-2\frac{1}{4})\div(-2\frac{3}{5})$ 5.5.121) $(-1\frac{6}{8})\div(2\frac{1}{2})$ 5.5.122) $(-3\frac{2}{3})\div(-1\frac{3}{5})$ 5.5.123) $(2\frac{1}{2})\div(-3\frac{1}{4})$

5.5.124) $(2)\div(-1\frac{3}{4})$ 5.5.125) $(-3)\div(-1\frac{1}{3})$ 5.5.126) $(-1)\div(\frac{5}{6})$ 5.5.127) $(2)\div(-1\frac{4}{5})$

5.5.128) $(-2\frac{1}{3})\div(-1)$ 5.5.129) $(-3\frac{1}{4})\div(-2)$ 5.5.130) $(-1\frac{2}{3})\div(-1)$ 5.5.131) $(-1\frac{3}{4})\div(2)$

5.5.w1) I have 1/3 of a pie and I divide it into 6 equal parts. How much of a pie does each piece have?

5.5.w2) If I have 1/6 pound of candy and want to divide it into 4 equal piles. How much does each pile have?

5.5.w3) If I cut a 34 foot rope into ¼ foot pieces. How many pieces will I have?

5.5.w4) When I practice math I do it for 4/5 hour each time. If last month I practiced for 12 hours how many hours did I practice?

Fraction reduction
Convert each improper fraction to a mixed fraction

5.5.132) 11/2	5.5.133) 4/3	5.5.134) 9/4	5.5.135) 12/4	5.5.136) 15/3	5.5.137) 13/2
5.5.138) 45/3	5.5.139) 21/7	5.5.140) 31/7	5.5.141) 75/5	5.5.142) 14/2	5.5.143) 32/8
5.5.144) 21/3	5.5.145) 76/6	5.5.146) 41/4	5.5.147) 65/7	5.5.148) 56/5	5.5.149) 79/4
5.5.150) 98/8	5.5.151) 17/5	5.5.152) 65/3	5.5.153) 86/4	5.5.154) 127/3	5.5.155) 67/6
5.5.156) 78/5	5.5.157) 14/4	5.5.158) 99/9	5.5.159) 165/3	5.5.160) 81/3	5.5.161) 145/8

5.5.192) 14/3	5.5.193) 27/2	5.5.194) 16/5	5.5.195) 19/3	5.5.196) 19/2	5.5.197) 59/4
5.5.198) 126/5	5.5.199) 87/4	5.5.200) 88/3	5.5.201) 21/5	5.5.202) 41/3	5.5.203) 61/5
5.5.204) 13/2	5.5.205) 25/3	5.5.206) 47/5	5.5.207) 23/2	5.5.208) 191/5	5.5.209) 91/6
5.5.210) 47/5	5.5.211) 57/2	5.5.212) 51/2	5.5.213) 71/6	5.5.214) 61/3	5.5.215) 39/2

Reduce fractions to reduced forms

5.5.162) 10/2	5.5.163) 12/3	5.5.164) 20/4	5.5.165) 4/12	5.5.166) 3/15	5.5.167) 6/12
5.5.168) 3/45	5.5.169) 7/21	5.5.170) 7/35	5.5.171) 5/75	5.5.172) 2/14	5.5.173) 8/32
5.5.174) 3/21	5.5.175) 6/78	5.5.176) 4/44	5.5.177) 7/49	5.5.178) 125/5	5.5.179) 4/14
5.5.180) 12/8	5.5.181) 6/18	5.5.182) 66/33	5.5.183) 88/4	5.5.184) 3/126	5.5.185) 6/16
5.5.186) 80/15	5.5.187) 14/4	5.5.188) 99/9	5.5.189) 3/165	5.5.190) 3/81	5.5.191) 8/168

Convert the Decimal to Fractions and Percent

5.7.1) 1.4	5.7.2) 6.1	5.7.3) 2.67	5.7.4) 3.45	5.7.5) 1.878	5.7.6) 9.35
5.7.7) 142.36	5.7.8) 2.25	5.7.9) 4.325	5.7.10) 13.45	5.7.11) 0.71	5.7.12) 7.66
5.7.13) 3.578	5.7.14) 0.0055	5.7.15) 0.37	5.7.16) 12.35	5.7.17) 0.32	5.7.18) 0.016
5.7.19) 11.3	5.7.20) 10	5.7.21) 2.7676	5.7.22) 6.257	5.7.23) 17.35	5.7.24) 6.3
5.7.25) 9.1	5.7.26) 3.46	5.7.27) 3.990	5.7.28) 1.01	5.7.29) 3.41	5.7.30) 0.125

Convert the Fractions to Decimals and Percent

5.8.1) $\frac{4}{100}$	5.8.2) $\frac{27}{100}$	5.8.3) $\frac{13}{1000}$	5.8.4) $\frac{3}{10}$	5.8.5) $\frac{67}{100}$	5.8.6) $\frac{12}{1000}$
5.8.7) $1\frac{27}{100}$	5.8.8) $\frac{3}{100}$	5.8.9) $2\frac{34}{1000}$	5.8.10) $1\frac{7}{10}$	5.8.11) $3\frac{4}{100}$	5.8.12) $1\frac{2}{1000}$
5.8.13) $\frac{6}{10}$	5.8.14) $2\frac{3}{10}$	5.8.15) $3\frac{5}{10}$	5.8.16) $\frac{4}{100}$	5.8.17) $4\frac{1}{100}$	5.8.18) $2\frac{47}{1000}$
5.8.19) $2\frac{137}{1000}$	5.8.20) $3\frac{4}{10}$	5.8.21) $16\frac{7}{10}$	5.8.22) $3\frac{3}{1000}$	5.8.23) $\frac{89}{100}$	5.8.24) $\frac{127}{100}$
5.8.25) $\frac{14}{100}$	5.8.26) $\frac{6}{1000}$	5.8.27) $\frac{29}{100}$	5.8.28) $\frac{9}{1000}$	5.8.29) $16\frac{23}{100}$	5.8.30) $1\frac{45}{1000}$

Convert the Fractions to Decimals and Percent (round decimals to the tenths place)

5.8.31) 4/6	5.8.32) 6/9	5.8.33) 2/3	5.8.34) 1/2	5.8.35) 8/7	5.8.36) 7/3
5.8.37) 3/4	5.8.38) 1/5	5.8.39) 2/7	5.8.40) 4/3	5.8.41) 1/6	5.8.42) 4/5
5.8.43) 4/7	5.8.44) 2/6	5.8.45) 2/9	5.8.46) 4/4	5.8.47) 8/6	5.8.48) 3/9
5.8.49) 7/5	5.8.50) 5/3	5.8.51) 3/6	5.8.52) 2/5	5.8.53) 2/2	5.8.54) 5/2
5.8.55) 6/4	5.8.56) 3/2	5.8.57) 3/7	5.8.58) 1/3	5.8.59) 5/4	5.8.60) 3/5

For one on one tutoring via skype at $35.00/Hr.; contact me at marksmathtutoring@yahoo.com

Convert the Percent to a Fraction and a decimal

5.8.61) 36%   5.8.62) 128%   5.8.63) 2%   5.8.64) 65%   5.8.65) 12%   5.8.66) 39%

5.8.67) 161%   5.8.68) 23%   5.8.69) 51%   5.8.70) 146%   5.8.71) 436%   5.8.72)225%

5.8.73) 87%   5.8.74) 177%   5.8.75) 218%   5.8.76) 4%   5.8.77) 169%   5.8.78) 47%

5.8.79) 301%   5.8.80) 259%   5.8.81) 326%   5.8.82) 269%   5.8.83) 251%   5.8.84) 78%

5.8.w1) If I buy a bag of cookies and 9/12 of them are chocolate. Which fraction below is equivalent to this fraction

a) 4/6   b) 3/3   c) 3/4   d) 5/8

Inequalities

State which symbol (<,>,≤,≥,=) best describes the relationship between the two fractions shown:

5.6.1) 1/2,2/2   5.6.2) 2/3,1/3   5.6.3) 5/6,7/6   5.6.4) 3/4,1/4

5.6.5) 5/8,7/8   5.6.6) 3/9,4/9   5.6.7) 4/5,3/5   5.6.8) 7/6,4/6

5.6.9) 3/9, 2/9   5.6.10) 4/7,6/7   5.6.11) 1/3,1/3   5.6.12) 4/6,4/6

5.6.13) 3/8,2/8   5.6.14) 2/7,1/7   5.6.15) 2/11,3/11   5.6.16) 8/16,4/16

5.6.17) 12/8,14/8   5.6.18) 3/7,5/7   5.6.19) 1/12,5/12   5.6.20) 5/13,7/13

5.6.21) 7/12,11/12   5.6.22) 8/15,5/15   5.6.23) 6/11,12/11   5.6.24) 7/10,4/10

5.6.25) 3/4,3/2   5.6.26) 2/3,2/5   5.6.27) 3/6,3/5   5.6.28) 3/4,3/8

5.6.29) 5/8,5/6   5.6.30) 6/9,6/10   5.6.31) 4/5,4/2   5.6.32) 5/6, 5/8

5.6.33) 3/9, 3/4   5.6.34) 4/7, 4/8   5.6.35) 1/3, 1/4   5.6.36) 4/6, 4/5

5.6.37) 3/8, 3/9   5.6.38) 4/7, 4/6   5.6.39) 2/11, 2/3   5.6.40) 5/16, 5/12

5.6.41) 12/8, 12/18   5.6.42) 3/7, 3/2   5.6.43) 6/12, 6/4   5.6.44) 5/13, 5/8

5.6.45) 7/12, 7/10   5.6.46) 8/15, 8/9   5.6.47) 6/11, 6/8   5.6.48) 7/10, 7/3

5.6.w9) If I sell 6 out of 8 cupcakes which fraction below best represents this fraction

a) 6/16

b) 12/16

c) 12/8

d) 1/2

Using <, >, ≤, ≥ to complete the following statements

5.6.66) 35, 51   5.6.67) 21, 68   5.6.68) 13, 54   5.6.69) 65, 89

5.6.70) 135, 21   5.6.71) 2134, 321   5.6.72) 12, 138   5.6.73) 789, 46

5.6.74) 533, 267   5.6.75) 887, 4567   5.6.76) 12, 476   5.6.77) 12.1, 33.7

5.6.78) 34, 34.2   5.6.79) 67.01, 67.1   5.6.80) 889.25, 889.2   5.6.81) 12.01, 13.01

5.6.82) 128.3, 128.03   5.6.83) 1.225, 1.252   5.6.84) 3.1, 4.5   5.6.85) 56.7, 65.7

State which symbol (<,>,≤,≥,=) best describes the relationship between the two fractions shown:

5.6.119)3/4,1/3   5.6.120)2/3,1/6   5.6.121)3/4,4/5   5.6.122)2/7,1/2

5.6.123)5/7,2/3   5.6.124)2/3,2/7   5.6.125)3/7,5/6   5.6.126)3/5,1/2

5.6.127)2/5,1/4   5.6.128)3/7,7/8   5.6.129)3/7,3/5   5.6.130)2/7,1/4

5.6.131)5/7,1/5   5.6.132)1/8,1/3   5.6.133)1/8,3/5   5.6.134)1/6,3/8

5.6.135)3/7,1/3   5.6.136)3/7,2/3   5.6.137)6/7,5/8   5.6.138)6/7,3/4

5.6.139)1/3,5/6   5.6.140)1/3,1/2   5.6.141)2/5,1/6   5.6.142)3/4,5/6

5.6.143)1/6,1/3   5.6.144)1/4,1/6   5.6.145)2/5,5/6   5.6.146)3/7,4/5

5.6.147)2/3,1/5   5.6.148)3/4,2/3   5.6.149)1/3,5/7   5.6.150)5/8,5/6

5.6.251)$1^2/_3, 2^1/_4$ 5.6.252)$2^1/_6, 2^3/_4$ 5.6.253)$3^1/_5, 1^1/_4$ 5.6.254)$2^1/_8, 1^1/_7$

5.6.255)$2^5/_8, 3^2/_5$ 5.6.256)$2^5/_8, 1^1/_3$ 5.6.257)$1^5/_7, 3^5/_6$ 5.6.258)$2^2/_7, 3^1/_2$

5.6.259)$1^3/_5, 2^3/_8$ 5.6.260) $1^3/_5, 2^6/_7$ 5.6.261) 1 ¼,$1^1/_3$ 5.6.262)$1^1/_3, 3^1/_5$

5.6.263)$1\,^2/_7, 4\,^1/_5$ 5.6.264) $1\,^4/_7, 3\,^2/_3$ 5.6.265) $1\,^5/_8, 2\,^4/_7$ 5.6.266)$2\,^1/_4, 2\,^5/_6$

5.6.267)$2\,\frac{1}{2}, 3\,^5/_7$ 5.6.268) $3\,^1/_7, 2\,^1/_6$ 5.6.269) $1\,^3/_8, 4\,^2/_3$ 5.6.270)$1\,^1/_6, 2\,^1/_5$

5.6.271)$2\,^4/_7, 2\,^2/_5$ 5.6.272)$1\,^2/_5, 1\,^1/_6$ 5.6.273)$2\,^7/_8, 2\,^1/_6$ 5.6.274)$1\,^2/_5, 3\,^7/_8$

5.6.275)$1\,^2/_7, 4\,^1/_5$ 5.6.276)$1\,^4/_7, 3\,^2/_3$ 5.6.277)$1\,^5/_8, 2\,^4/_7$ 5.6.278)$2\,\frac{1}{4}, 2\,^5/_8$

5.6.279)$2\,^5/_8, 3\,^4/_5$ 5.6.280)$2\,^1/_4, 2\,^4/_5$ 5.6.281)$1\,^4/_5, 3\,^6/_7$ 5.6.282)$1\,^3/_8, 2\,^3/_7$

5.6.283) $3, 2\,^3/_7$ 5.6.284) $1, 6\,^5/_8$ 5.6.285) $5, 8\,^7/_8$ 5.6.286) $8, 3\,^1/_6$

5.6.287) $9, 2\,^5/_8$ 5.6.288) $9\,^8/_9, 4$ 5.6.289)$3, 1\,^2/_9$ 5.6.290)$5\,^3/_7, 4$

5.6.291) $4, 2\,^3/_5$ 5.6.292) $2\,^4/_7, 6$ 5.6.293) $1, 8\,^2/_9$ 5.6.294)$2\,^4/_9, 7$

5.6.w1) If four friends bought a box of cookies each the table show how many were chocolate.

FRIEND	CHOCOLATE
Mike	2/5
Mary	3/10
Sue	5/20
David	11/40

Which person had the highest fraction of chocolate cookies?

5.6.w2) If the box of cookies had 6/10 chocolate which statement below is true
a) out of 100 cookies 6 were chocolate
b) out of 20 cookies 15 were chocolate
c) out of 15 cookies 9 were chocolate
d) out of 40 cookies 25 were chocolate

5.6.w3) I ate 38/54 cookies in one day. Which fraction below is the same fraction
a) 19/27   b) 6/9   c) 2/3   d) 12/15

5.6.w4) If I drink 3/5 of a bottle of water which fraction below is greater than 3/5
a) 5/10   b) 4/7   c) 9/14   d) 1/3

5.6.w5) I count the kinds of fish in a tank. The results are shown in the table below.

FISH TYPE	FRACTION
Guppy	2/5
Angle	3/10
Sword	1/10
Gold	1/5

Which fish has the largest population in the tank

5.6.w6) I finish 35 out of 60 math problems in my homework. Which fraction below is **NOT** the same fraction
a) 7/12   b) 70/120   c) 57/90   d) 105/180

5.6.w7) I read 4/6 of a book. What fraction below is equivalent to this fraction
a) 8/13   b) 11/18   c) 2/3   d) 13/24

5.6.w8) I spend 2/5 of an hour mowing the lawn. Which fraction below is less than this
a) 4/10   b) 5/15   c) 2/3   d) 8/20

5.10.w1) The model below represents the number $1\,{}^{13}/_{100}$

Which stamen below represents the same value

a) 1.87
b) 1.13
c) 1.15
d) 1.31

5.10.w2) The model below $1\,{}^{4}/_{100}$

Which decimal represents the same value
a) 1.4
b) 1.04
c) 1.44
d) 4.01

5.10.w3) The drawing below is colored to show a fraction

Which statement below explains this drawing
a) ${}^{2}/_{3}$
b) $2\,{}^{2}/_{3}$
c) 2 ¾
d) $2\,{}^{2}/_{4}$

 Croquis of a
Deliberate
Crime

YouTube

5.10.w4) The drawing below is colored to show a fraction

Which of the following best represents this fraction
a) $^1/_8$
b) ¾
c) 1 ¾
d) 1 $^1/_8$

5.10.w5) The drawing below has been colored to represent a number

Which number below best represents this drawing?
a) $^6/_{10}$ or 0.6
b) 2 $^6/_{10}$ or 2.6
c) 2 $^4/_{10}$ or 2.4
d) 1 $^4/_{10}$ or 1.4

5.10.w6) The drawing below has been colored to show a number

Which of the numbers below best represents this number
a) $^2/_{10}$ or 0.2
b) 1 $^2/_{10}$ or 1.2
c) 1 $^8/_{10}$ or 1.8
d) $^8/_{10}$ or 0.8

5.10.w7) The drawing below has been colored to show a number

Which of the numbers below best represents this number
a) $^7/_{10}$ or 0.7
b) $^5/_{10}$ or 0.5
c) 1 $^3/_5$ or 1.6
d) $^3/_5$ or 0.3

Croquis of a
Deliberate
Crime

YouTube

5.10.w8) The drawing below has been colored to show a number

Which of the numbers below best represents this number
a) $1^5/_{10}$ or 1.5
b) $^5/_{10}$ or 0.5
c) $1^4/_5$ or 1.8
d) $^3/_5$ or 0.6

5.10.w9) The drawing below is colored to represent a number

Which stamen below best describes this number in words
a) one and seven hundredths
b) six hundredths
c) ninety four hundredths
d) one and ninety four hundredths

5.10.w10)The drawing below is colored to represent a number

Which stamen below best describes this number in words
a) three and twenty five hundredths
b) fifteen hundredths
c) three hundreds and fifteen
d) eighty five hundredth

5.10.w11) The drawing below is colored to represent a number

Which statement below best describes this number in words
a) three sixths
b) four sixth
c) two tenths
d) four tenths

Croquis of a
Deliberate
Crime

YouTube

For one on one tutoring via skype at $35.00/Hr.; contact me at marksmathtutoring@yahoo.com

5.10.w12) The drawing below is colored to represent a number

Which statement below best describes this number in words
a) five eights
b) three eights
c) two and three eights
d) two and three tenths

5.10.w13) The drawing below is colored to represent a number

Which statement below best describes this number in words
a) one thirds
b) two and two thirds
c) two and one third
d) two thirds

5.10.w14) The drawing below is colored to represent a number

Which statement below best describes this number in words
a) seven tenths
b) two and seven tenths
c) two and seven hundredths
d) two and three tenths

5.10.w15) The drawing below is colored to represent a number

Which statement below best describes this number in words
a) three tenths
b) one and seven tenths
c) one and three tenths
d) two tenths

Croquis of a
Deliberate
Crime
YouTube

If you don't get the correct answer, and want an explanation on how to work the problem, go to YouTube and type in "MMT" then the problem number. An example would be, MMT 3.9.w12,. The video will show you how to work problem 3.9.w12.

5.10.w16) The drawing below is shaded to represent a number

a)   b)   c)   d)

Which of the following represents these drawing in decimal form

a) 0.37, 0.45, 076, 0.89

b) 0.08, 0.25, 0.34, 0.58

c) 0.8, 0.25, 0.34, 0.58

d) 0.08, 0.05, 0.04, 0.08

5.10.w17) The drawing below is shaded to represent a number

a)   b)   c)   d)

Which of the following represents these drawing in decimal form

a) 0.1, 0.3, 0.6, 0.9

b) 0.01, 0.03, 0. 06, 0.09

c) 1.1, 3.3, 6.6, 9.9

d) 1.9, 3.7, 6.4, 9.1

5.10.w18) Which diagram below represents the fraction 67/100

a)   c)

b)   d)

5.10.w19)The drawing below has been colored to represent the fraction $2\,{}^{6}/_{10}$

Which decimal best represents this number?

a) 1.4

b) 2.6

c) 0.6

d) 0.4

For one on one tutoring via skype at $35.00/Hr.; contact me at marksmathtutoring@yahoo.com

5.10.w20)Which of the following represents the same fraction

a)

c)

b)

d)

5.10.w21) Which of the following represents the fraction 6/10
a) 0.06
b) 0.6
c) 1.6
d) 1.06

5.10.w22) Which of the following represents the fraction 85/100
a) 1.85
b) 0.85
c) 85.0
d) 8.5

5.10.w23) If my dog weights 0.37 KG what is this in a fraction
a) $^{37}/_{10}$
b) $^{37}/_{100}$
c) $3 \, ^{7}/_{100}$
d) $^{37}/_{1000}$

5.10.w24) Which of the following are equivalent?
a) 27/100=0.027
b) 1/10=0.01
c) 13/1000=0.013
d) 25/100=0.025

5.10.w25) Which of the following best represents them fraction $3 \, ^{12}/_{100}$
a) 3.12
b) 312.100
c) 3.012
d)0.0312

Croquis of a
Deliberate
Crime

YouTube

If you don't get the correct answer, and want an explanation on how to work the problem, go to YouTube and type in "MMT" then the problem number. An example would be, MMT 3.9.w12,. The video will show you how to work problem 3.9.w12.

6.0 GRAPHING

6.1)The graph below shows the number of cookies your brother ate.

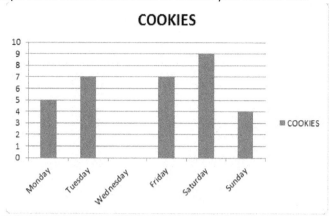

If the total of cookies eaten was 36, how many cookies were eaten on Wednesday?

6.2) What is the total weight of all the dogs shown in the graph below?

Croquis of a Deliberate Crime
YouTube

If you don't get the correct answer, and want an explanation on how to work the problem, go to YouTube and type in "MMT" then the problem number. An example would be, MMT 3.9.w12,. The video will show you how to work problem 3.9.w12.

For one on one tutoring via skype at $35.00/Hr.; contact me at marksmathtutoring@yahoo.com

6.3) Given the graph below

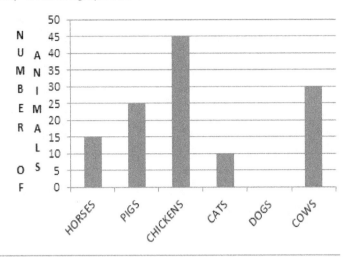

If there are 140 animals total on this farm which graph below indicated the number of cats

a)   b)   c)   d)

6.4) The following table describes the number of fruit trees on a farm

Type of fruit tree	Number of trees
Apple	11,256
Pear	8,765
Plum	12,367
Cherry	10,018
Peach	9,672

Which stamen is not true based on the data in the above table
a)Apples>Pear, b) Plums>Cherry, c) Peach<Cherry, d) Plum<Apple

Croquis of a Deliberate Crime

YouTube

If you don't get the correct answer, and want an explanation on how to work the problem, go to YouTube and type in "MMT" then the problem number. An example would be, MMT 3.9.w12,. The video will show you how to work problem 3.9.w12.

For one on one tutoring via skype at $35.00/Hr.; contact me at marksmathtutoring@yahoo.com

6.5) The graph below indicates the number of cars of each type for sale at a lot.

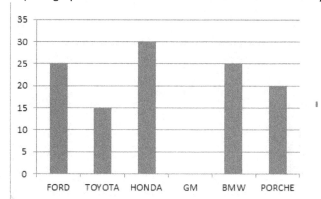

If there are 135 cars total on the lot for sale which graph below shows the number of GMs

a)   b)   c)   d)

6.6) The graph below shows the number of tons of garbage collected by the city per month

	X			
	X		X	
X	X		X	X
X	X	X	X	X
X	X	X	X	X
May	June	July	Aug	May

Each **X** represented 500 pounds

Based on the graph above how many more pounds of garbage did the city collect in August than May?

6.7) The table below details the number of games for each sport

SPORT	NUMBER
SOCCER	35
FOOTBALL	17
BASEBALL	176
BASKETBALL	125

Based on the information in the table organize the sports from high to low
a) baseball, soccer, basketball, football
b) baseball, basketball, soccer, football
c) football, soccer, basketball, baseball
d) basketball, baseball, football, soccer

If you don't get the correct answer, and want an explanation on how to work the problem, go to YouTube and type in "MMT" then the problem number. An example would be, MMT 3.9.w12,. The video will show you how to work problem 3.9.w12.

6.8) The following table details the number of minutes Mike did choirs.

		X	
X		X	
X		X	
X	X	X	X
X	X	X	X

Mon.　Tues.　Wed.　Thur.

Each X represents 10 minutes of work

How many more minutes of work did Mike do on Mon compared to Thur.?

6.9) The following table describes the number of different types of fish 4 kids have in their aquariums.

AQUARIUM	GUPPIES	ANGLES
Mary	12	4
Steve	15	5
Susan	21	7
Mark	9	3

Which statement below is correct based on the information in the tables

a) There are three time the number of guppies as angles

b) There are eight more guppies than angle

c) There are three time the number of angles as guppies

d) There is no relationship in the number of guppies and angles.

6.10) The following graph describes the number of kids in each grade who bring a sandwich to school for lunch.

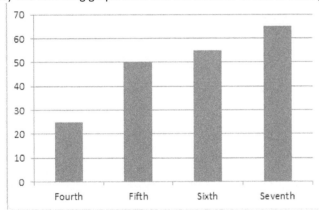

Based on the table above which statement is true

a) A total of 65 kids from the fourth and fifth grades had sandwiches

b) No grade brought 55 sandwiches

c) A total of 195 kids brought sandwiches

d) The difference between the seventh and fifth grades who brought sandwiches is 15

Croquis of a
Deliberate
Crime

YouTube

If you don't get the correct answer, and want an explanation on how to work the problem, go to YouTube and type in "MMT" then the problem number. An example would be, MMT 3.9.w12,. The video will show you how to work problem 3.9.w12.

6.11) The following table details the amount of a discount a store is giving based on the amount you buy.

AMOUNT OF PURCHASE	AMOUNT AFTER DISCOUNT
$23.00	$18.00
$28.00	$23.00
$33.00	$28.00
$38.00	$33.00
$43.00	$38.00

Based on the information given in the table which statement is true
a) The amount after discount minus $5.00 equals the amount of purchase
b) There is no relationship between the two values
c) The amount after discount minus $5.00 equals the amount of purchase
d) The amount after discount is always $5.00 less than the amount of purchase

6.12)The following table describes the number of kids with each name in a school

NAMES	NUMBERS
Mike	35
James	25
John	15
Elmer	40

Which table below describes this data best

A)

NAMES	NUMBERS
Mike	XXXXXXX
James	XXXXX
John	XXXX
Elmer	XXXXXXXX

Each X is equal to 5 students

C)

NAMES	NUMBERS
Mike	XXXXXX
James	XXXXX
John	XXXXX
Elmer	XXXXXXXX

Each X is equal to 5 students

B)

NAMES	NUMBERS
Mike	XXXXXXX
James	XXXXX
John	XXX
Elmer	XXXXXXXX

Each X is equal to 5 students

D)

NAMES	NUMBERS
Mike	XXXXXXXX
James	XXXXX
John	XXX
Elmer	XXXXXXX

Each X is equal to 5 students

Croquis of a Deliberate Crime

YouTube

If you don't get the correct answer, and want an explanation on how to work the problem, go to YouTube and type in "MMT" then the problem number. An example would be, MMT 3.9.w12,. The video will show you how to work problem 3.9.w12.

For one on one tutoring via skype at $35.00/Hr.; contact me at marksmathtutoring@yahoo.com

6.13) The following graph describes the number of hamburger I ate each weekday.

Which of the following tables best represents this data

a)

DAY	Mon	Tue	Wed	Thur	Fri
NUMBER	3	5	6	4	6

c)

DAY	Mon	Tue	Wed	Thur	Fri
NUMBER	3	5	4	6	4

b)

DAY	Mon	Tue	Wed	Thur	Fri
NUMBER	3	6	5	7	5

d)

DAY	Mon	Tue	Wed	Thur	Fri
NUMBER	3	7	4	7	5

6.14) The following table details the number of fish dinner a resturant sales

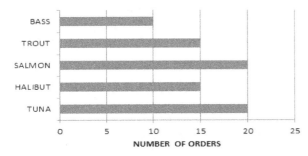

Which of the following tables best describes the data in the graph above

A)

FISH DINNER	NUMBER
BASS	10
TROUT	20
SLAMON	15
HALIBUT	15
TUNA	20

C)

FISH DINNER	NUMBER
BASS	10
TROUT	15
SLAMON	20
HALIBUT	15
TUNA	20

B)

FISH DINNER	NUMBER
BASS	10
TROUT	15
SLAMON	20
HALIBUT	25
TUNA	20

D)

FISH DINNER	NUMBER
BASS	10
TROUT	15
SLAMON	20
HALIBUT	15
TUNA	10

For one on one tutoring via skype at $35.00/Hr.; contact me at marksmathtutoring@yahoo.com

6.15) The following graph details the number of books I read per year I read

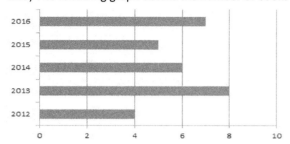

Which of the following tables best represents this data

A)

YEAR	NUMBER
2016	7
2015	5
2014	6
2013	8
2012	4

C)

YEAR	NUMBER
2016	7
2015	5
2014	8
2013	6
2012	4

B)

YEAR	NUMBER
2016	7
2015	5
2014	8
2013	8
2012	4

D)

YEAR	NUMBER
2016	7
2015	5
2014	6
2013	8
2012	6

6.16) The following tables describes the number of times a number was picked at randon from the deck of cards

DAY OF THE WEEK	NUMBER OF TIMES
One	4
Two	6
Three	5
Four	4
Five	3
Six	2

A)

C)

B)

D)

Croquis of a
Deliberate
Crime

YouTube

6.17) The following table details the number of miles I ran in one day

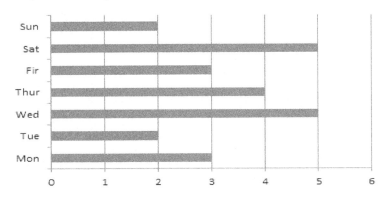

Which table below best describes this data?

A)

DAY	MILES
MON	3
TUE	2
WED	4
THUR	5
FRI	3
SAT	5
SUN	2

C)

DAY	MILES
MON	2
TUE	5
WED	3
THUR	4
FRI	5
SAT	2
SUN	3

B)

DAY	MILES
MON	3
TUE	2
WED	5
THUR	4
FRI	3
SAT	5
SUN	3

D)

DAY	MILES
MON	3
TUE	2
WED	5
THUR	4
FRI	3
SAT	5
SUN	2

6.18) The following list of numbers represents the card that was pulled from a deck.
   3,2,7,6,6,7,5,10,2,3,7,3,7,1,3,
Which dot diagram below best represents this data

Croquis of a
Deliberate
Crime

YouTube

For one on one tutoring via skype at $35.00/Hr.; contact me at marksmathtutoring@yahoo.com

6.19) Based on the graph below, how many more chocolate cupcakes were sold than vanilla

a) 5
b) 4
c) 6
d) 8

6.20) The graph below shows the number of fruits a grocery has on the shelf. Based on the this information how many more oranges than pears does the grocery have

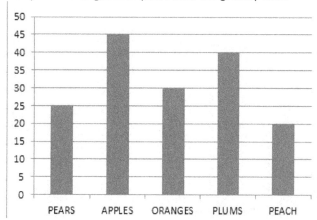

6.21) The graph below shows the number of hours I spent playing with my dog and cat.

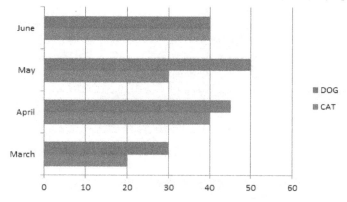

Based on this graph how many more hours in April did I play with my dog vs my cat?

For one on one tutoring via skype at $35.00/Hr.; contact me at marksmathtutoring@yahoo.com

6.22) The graph below show the number of cookies I are in each weekday.

If I want to eat the same number of cookies each day how many more should I eat on Tues to equal the number I arte oh Wed?

6.23) The graph below shows the amount of money I earned mowing lawns and washing cars for four months.

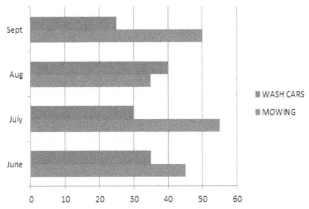

What is the difference in the amount of money I earned mowing lawns than washing cars?

6.24) The following graph shows the number of fish I caught each day during the summer.

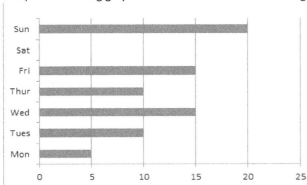

If I caught a total of 85 fish, how many must I have caught on Sat?

Croquis of a
Deliberate
Crime

YouTube

For one on one tutoring via skype at $35.00/Hr.; contact me at marksmathtutoring@yahoo.com

6.25) The following is a list of the length in inches of the fish I caught this summer.

            12,14,16,12,18,22,16,24,16,18,13,23

Which of the table below best represents this data

a)

c)

steam	leaf
1	2, 4, 6, 6, 6, 8
2	2, 3, 4

b)

d)

steam	leaf
1	2, 4, 6, 8
2	2, 3, 4
3	0

6.26) The following table list the amount of fruit a farmer produced last year

FRUIT TYPE	NUMBER
Apples	125,835,266
Pears	217,346,893
Oranges	187,663,524
Peaches	237,894,332
Plums	109,475,872

Based on the information in this table which list below organizes this data from lowest to highest.
a) Plums, Oranges, Apples, Pears, Peaches
b) Plums, Apples, Oranges, Pears, Peaches
c) Peaches, Pears, Oranges, Apples, Plums
d) Plums, Apples, Oranges, Peaches, Pears

6.27) The following table list the number of fish I caught this summer based on their type.

FISH TYPE	NUMBER
Bass	45
Trout	
Salmon	17

If I caught a total of 63 fish how many Trout must I have caught?

6.28)The steam and leaf plot shown below show the weights of dogs in my neighborhood.

steam	leaf
1	3, 6, 8, 8
2	2, 6
3	5,5,8
4	1,5
5	0, 6, 7

Based on the information in this table what is the difference between the lightest and the heaviest dog?

For one on one tutoring via skype at $35.00/Hr.; contact me at marksmathtutoring@yahoo.com

6.29) The following two pictures detail the size of my friends back yards

Mary

Sam

Susan

Mike

List these numbers in order of highest to lowest
a) 1.6, 1.46, 1.3, 1.2
b) 1.2, 1.3, 1.46, 1.6
c) 1.46, 1.6, 1.3, 1.2
d) 1.2, 1.3, 1.6, 1.46

6.30) Given the information in the table below

WEIGHT	½	1	1 ½	2	2 ½	3	3 ½	4
NUMBER	2	4	0	3	6	2	1	4

a)

b)

c)

d)

Croquis of a
Deliberate
Crime

YouTube

For one on one tutoring via skype at $35.00/Hr.; contact me at marksmathtutoring@yahoo.com

6.31)The following table illustrates the number of biscuits my dog can eat for a specific number of hours

NUMBER OF HOURS	NUMBER OF BUSCUITS
1	15
2	30
3	45

A)

B)

C)

D)

6.32) Given the graph below which table best represents this data.

A)

HOURS	POUNDS
1	2
2	4
3	6
4	8

B)

HOURS	POUNDS
1	2
3	4
5	6
6	8

C)

HOURS	POUNDS
1	3
2	6
3	9
4	12

D)

HOURS	POUNDS
1	4
2	8
3	12
4	16

6.33) Which of the following points has the coordinates of (7,3)

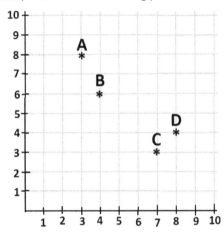

6.34) What is the coordinates of the point in the graph below

Croquis of a
Deliberate
Crime
YouTube

For one on one tutoring via skype at $35.00/Hr.; contact me at marksmathtutoring@yahoo.com

6.35) which point has the coordinates of (2,7)

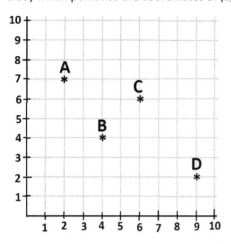

6.36) Which coordinate is **NOT** on the line of the graph below

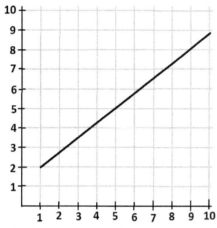

A) (5,5)
B)(9,8)
C) (2,2)
D) (3,4)

Croquis of a
Deliberate
Crime

YouTube

If you don't get the correct answer, and want an explanation on how to work the problem, go to YouTube and type in "MMT" then the problem number. An example would be, MMT 3.9.w12,. The video will show you how to work problem 3.9.w12.

For one on one tutoring via skype at $35.00/Hr.; contact me at marksmathtutoring@yahoo.com

6.37) Which of the graphs below best represent the data presented in the following table

X	Y
2	5
8	6
9	8
10	10

A)

B)

C)

D)

6.38) I measured the weight of my new puppy and recorded the results in the table below

     #First week she gained 2 pound

     # each week after that she gained 3 pounds

Which graph below shows this data

A)

B)

C)

D)

For one on one tutoring via skype at $35.00/Hr.; contact me at marksmathtutoring@yahoo.com

6.39) Given the information in the graph below

Which table below best describes this information

A)

X	1/3	2/3	5/3
Y	2/3	4/3	5/3

B)

X	1/3	2/3	5/3
Y	2/3	5/3	4/3

C)

X	1/3	2/3	4/3
Y	2/3	2/3	5/3

D)

X	1/3	2/3	4/3
Y	2/3	4/3	5/3

6.40) The following table show the number of soda pops sold vs atterndence at the theam park

TEMPERATURE	SODAS SOLD
75	20
80	40
85	30
90	70
95	50
100	80

A)

B)

C)

D)

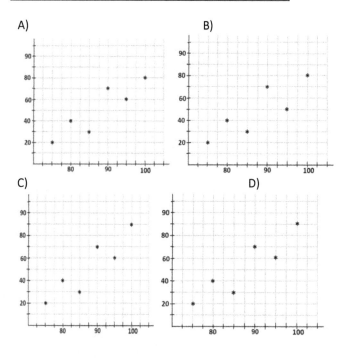

For one on one tutoring via skype at $35.00/Hr.; contact me at marksmathtutoring@yahoo.com

6.41) Given The graph below

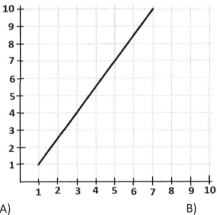

A)

X	1	3	5	7
Y	3	4	7	11

B)

X	1	3	5	7
Y	3	5	7	10

C)

X	1	3	5	7
Y	3	4	8	10

D)

X	1	3	5	7
Y	1	4	7	10

6.42) Which table blow represents the data presented in this graph

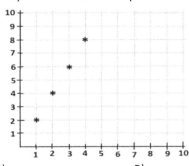

A)

X	Y
1	2
2	5
3	6
4	8

B)

X	Y
1	2
2	4
3	6
4	8

C)

X	Y
1	2
2	4
3	5
4	8

D)

X	Y
1	2
2	4
3	6
4	7

6.43) In the order pair (3,4) what is the value of X

Croquis of a Deliberate Crime

YouTube

6.44)Given the graph below

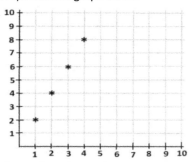

What is the relationship between each point?
A) Multiplication, each X is multiplied by 3 to get Y
B) Addition, each X is added to 1 to get Y
C) Multiplication each X is multiplied by 2 to get Y
D) Addition, each X is added to 1 to get Y

**Croquis of a
Deliberate
Crime**

YouTube

If you don't get the correct answer, and want an explanation on how to work the problem, go to YouTube and type in "MMT" then the problem number. An example would be, MMT 3.9.w12,. The video will show you how to work problem 3.9.w12.

For one on one tutoring via skype at $35.00/Hr.; contact me at marksmathtutoring@yahoo.com

7.0 MEASURMENTS

7.1) Use a ruler to measure in centimeters the two arrows below. What is the difference in their heights

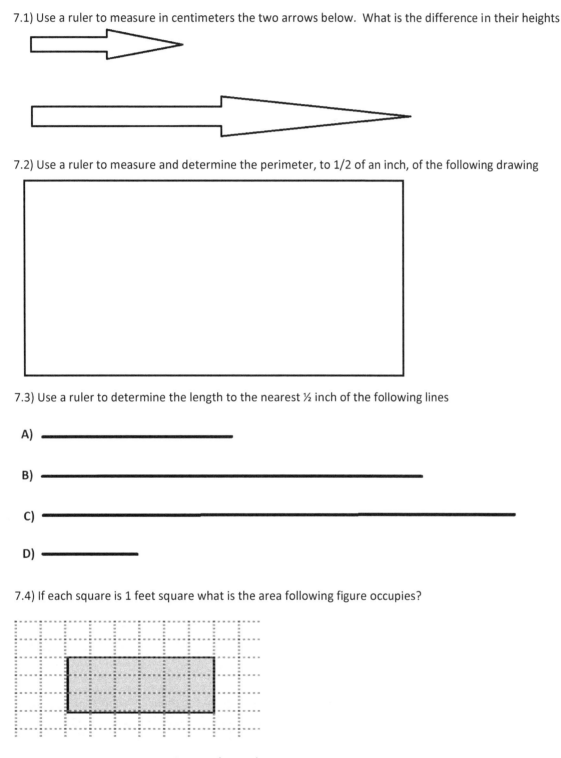

7.2) Use a ruler to measure and determine the perimeter, to 1/2 of an inch, of the following drawing

7.3) Use a ruler to determine the length to the nearest ½ inch of the following lines

A) ━━━━━━━━━━━

B) ━━━━━━━━━━━━━━━

C) ━━━━━━━━━━━━   ━━━━━━━━━━━

D) ━━━━━

7.4) If each square is 1 feet square what is the area following figure occupies?

For one on one tutoring via skype at $35.00/Hr.; contact me at marksmathtutoring@yahoo.com

7.5) What is the difference in inches between the length of these two figures. Your answer should be to the ½ inch.

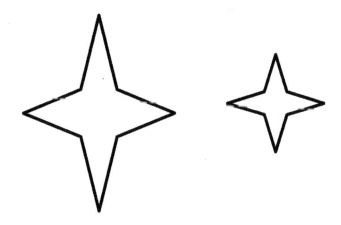

7.6) My mom placed a turkey in the oven at 1:45. 30 minutes later she put a pie in the same oven. She cooked both at the same time for 45 minutes. What time did she take both the turkey and pie from the oven?

7.7) On a fishing trip your family catches 50 fish then throws 15 back. Which number lone would be best in determining the number of fish your family kept.

7.8) Michelle studies math from 3:15 p.m. to 6:45 p.m. Which clock shows a time that she would be studying.

Croquis of a
Deliberate
Crime

YouTube

\# If you don't get the correct answer, and want an explanation on how to work the problem, go to YouTube and type in "MMT" then the problem number. An example would be, MMT 3.9.w12,. The video will show you how to work problem 3.9.w12.

\# For one on one tutoring via skype at $35.00/Hr.; contact me at marksmathtutoring@yahoo.com

7.9) The two clocks below show what time I started jogging and them stopped

STARTED   FINISHED

Which digital clock below shows a time of day I would have been jogging

a)   b)   c)   d)

 4:35   6:45   3:35   11:45

7.10) Mom put a turkey and a pie in the oven. They both went in at 4:15. The pie finished at 5:30. The turkey went an additional 45 minutes. Which clock below show the time the turkey was finished?

a)   b)   c)   d)

7.11) which letter best represents a point at 115?

7.12) Which number best represents the dot in the plot below

a) 4, b) 5, c) $4\frac{1}{2}$ d) $5\frac{1}{2}$

7.13) Which thermometer below show the temperature of 69°F

a)   b)   c)   d)

7.14) What Is the temperature shown below   7.15) What is the temperature shown below

7.16) What is the temperature shown below

7.17) What is the temperature shown below

7.18) what is the value of the point in the diagram below

a) $6^1/_4$, b) $6^3/_4$, c) $5^3/_4$, d) $5^1/_4$

7.19) Given the number line below,

200   300

Which stament below is correct
a) The dot has a value is more than 300
b) The dot has a value of less than 200
c) The dot has a value closer to 300 than 200
d) The dot has a value closer to 200 than 300

7.20) Given the number line below

13   14   15   16

The is the correct value of the dot
a) $14^1/_4$, b) $15^3/_4$, c) $14^3/_4$, d) $15^1/_4$

7.21) Which number line best represents the value of ½ foot
a)

0 foot   1 foot

c)

0 foot   1 foot

b)

0 foot   1 foot

d)

0 foot   1 foot

7.22) What number best represents the dot on the following diagram

125   175   300

a) 275, b) 325, c) 225, d) 250

7.23) What are the vaues of the dots shown on the ruler below

a) A=6, B=$7^1/_2$, C=$9^3/_4$
b) A=6, B=$7^1/_2$, C=$9^1/_4$
c) A=$6^1/_2$, B=$7^1/_2$, C=$9^3/_4$
d) A=6, B=$6^1/_2$, C=$9^1/_4$

7.24) The dot on the following number line represents a fraction

Which of the follwing number lines represents the same fraction

a)

c)

b)

d)

7.25) Which letter on the diagram below best represtents the number 243?

a) A
b) B
c) C
d) D

7.26) Which letter in the diagram below best represtnes the number 18 $^3/_4$

a) M
b) N
c) O
d) P

7.27) The R on the number line below is what value?

a) 13 ½
b) 12 ¾
c) 13 ¾
d) 12 ½

Croquis of a
Deliberate
Crime

YouTube

7.28) What iis the best value for the letter R in the number line below?

683   691   731

a) 719
b) 715
c) 723
d) 727

7.29) The letter U in the diagram below best representes what number?

13.6   14.2   16.1

a) 15.1
b) 14.9
c) 14.7
d) 15.2

7.30) The letter T in the number line below beast represents what number

31   33

a) 32
b) 32.1
c) 31.9
d) 31.8

7.31) What is the value of this angle?

a) 70 degrees
b) 20 degrees
c) 50 degrees
d) 110 degress

7.32) What is the value of this angle?

a) 55 degrees
b) 125 degrees
c) 135 degrees
d) 45 degrees

For one on one tutoring via skype at $35.00/Hr.; contact me at marksmathtutoring@yahoo.com

7.34) What is the value of this angle?

a) 50 degrees
b) 130 degrees
c) 45 degrees
d) 135 degress

7.35) What is the value of this angle?

a) 75 degrees
b) 165 degrees
c) 95 degrees
d) 40 degrees

7.36) What is the value of this angle?

a) 90 degrees
b) 125 degrees
c) 135 degrees
d) 190 degress

7.37) What is the value of this angle?

a) 65 degrees
b) 155 degrees
c) 90 degrees
d) 25 degrees

7.38) What is the value of this angle?

a) 0 degrees
b) 30 degrees
c) 130 degrees
d) 150 degress

7.39) What is the value of this angle?

a) 65 degrees
b) 0 degrees
c) 40 degrees
d) 140 degrees

Croquis of a
Deliberate
Crime

YouTube

For one on one tutoring via skype at $35.00/Hr.; contact me at marksmathtutoring@yahoo.com

7.40) What is the value of this angle?

7.41) What is the value of this angle?

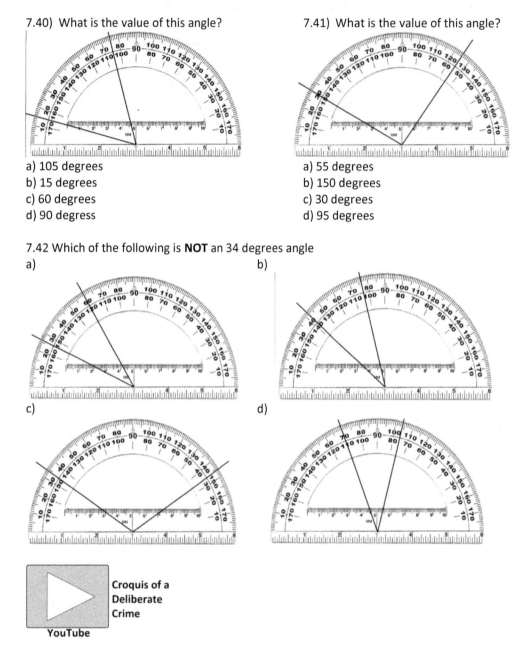

a) 105 degrees
b) 15 degrees
c) 60 degrees
d) 90 degress

a) 55 degrees
b) 150 degrees
c) 30 degrees
d) 95 degrees

7.42 Which of the following is **NOT** an 34 degrees angle

a)

b)

c)

d)

Croquis of a Deliberate Crime

YouTube

If you don't get the correct answer, and want an explanation on how to work the problem, go to YouTube and type in "MMT" then the problem number. An example would be, MMT 3.9.w12,. The video will show you how to work problem 3.9.w12.

For one on one tutoring via skype at $35.00/Hr.; contact me at marksmathtutoring@yahoo.com

7.43) 7.42 Which of the following is **NOT** an 67 degrees angle

a)   c)

b)   d)

7.44) Use a ruler, what is the perimiter of this draqwing to ½ inch

7.45) Use a ruler to measure the perimiters of the two following shapes. What is the difference in their perimiters to ½ inch?

7.46) What is the temp shown below?   7.47) What is the temp shown below?

For one on one tutoring via skype at $35.00/Hr.; contact me at marksmathtutoring@yahoo.com

7.48) Use a ruler. What is the length on the line drawn below in centimeters to ½ centimeter?

7.49) Use a ruler. What is the length on the line drawn below in centimeters to ½ centimeter?

7.50) Use a ruler. What is the length on the line drawn below in centimeters to ½ centimeter?

7.51) If I start sleeping when the clock reads as below

If I want to sleep for 1 hour and 45 minutes what time should I wake up

7.52) I I start walking at the following time

d)

If I want to walk for 2 hours and 35 minutes what time will I stop.

7.53) If I want to stop reading that the time shown below

d)

If I want to read for 1 hour and 50 minutes what time should I start

7.54) If I finish fishing at the time shown below

c)

If I want to fish for 2 hours and 50 minutes what time should I start

For one on one tutoring via skype at $35.00/Hr.; contact me at marksmathtutoring@yahoo.com

7.55) If I start cleaning at the time shown below.

a)

If I want to clean house for 3 hours and 30 minutes, what time will I fininsh

7.56) If I want to do something and start at the time shown below

c)

If I do it for 2 hours and 45 minutes what time will I finish

Croquis of a
Deliberate
Crime

YouTube

If you don't get the correct answer, and want an explanation on how to work the problem, go to YouTube and type in "MMT" then the problem number. An example would be, MMT 3.9.w12,. The video will show you how to work problem 3.9.w12.

For one on one tutoring via skype at $35.00/Hr.; contact me at marksmathtutoring@yahoo.com

8.0 STATS

8.1) Roger has marbles in a bag, with the following colors and quantities.

COLOR	QUANTITY
Red	10
Blue	15
Green	10
White	5
Brown	20

If Roger picks a marble at random what are the odds of it being a Red one
a) 10 in 60, b) 10 in 50, c) 50 in 60, d) 15 in 60

8.2) Given the diagram below

□ □ □ □ ○
□ □ □ □ ○

If I pick a shape at random without looking what are the odds it will be a square
a) 8 out of 10, b) 2 out of 10, c) 3 out of 5, d) 2 out of 5

8.3) Given the table below describing the types of cookies in a box

COOKIE TYPE	QUANTITY
Sugar	17
Oatmeal	15
Chocolate	20
Mint	17
Cinnamon	13

If I pick a cookie at random without looking what two types of cookies will have the same odds of being picked?

8.4) Pam has 18 brown marbles, 12 Green marbles, and 21 white marbles in a bag. If she chooses one at random without looking which statement below is true?
a) She will pick a brown one for sure
b) She is less likely to pick a Green one than a Brown
c) She is more likely to pick a Brown than a White
d) It is impossible to pick a Green marble

8.5) If I have 10 chocolate and 20 vanilla cupcakes in a box If I pick one at random what are the odds of it being chocolate

8.6) If I pick a day of the week at random, what are the odds it will be a weekend?

8.7)If I have 4 green, 6 brown, and 2 white marbles in a bag. I choose one without looking, what are the odds of it being a brown.

8.8) There are 56 girls and 49 boys in school. One has a secret. What are the odds it is a boy

8.9) There are 24 dogs in your neighborhood. One of them gets into the trash. What are the odds it is your dog.

8.10) If the lake has 112 bass, and 45 catfish what are the odds of catching a bass.

8.11) If there are 6 cokes and 8 sprits in the cooler. I pick one at random what are the odds of it being a coke.

8.12) If you made a 100% on a test with 12 questions, and your parents pick one problems to show them you can do it, what are the odds it will be one you got correct.

8.13) If your brother had two friends over to play baseball. One of them threw the ball and broke a window. What are the odds it was your brother

8.14) What are the odds the days you read this question is a weekday

8.15) Given the graph below what is the mean, median, and mode

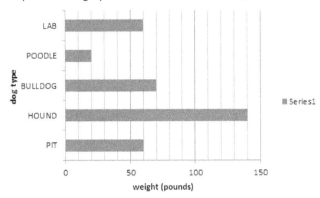

8.16) Given the table below what is the mean, median, and mode

SPORT	NUMBER
SOCCER	35
FOOTBALL	17
BASEBALL	176
BASKETBALL	125

8.17) Given the graph below what is the mean, median, mode

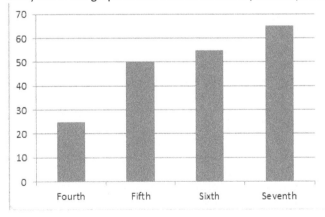

8.18) Given the table below what is the mean, median, and mode

NAMES	NUMBERS
Mike	35
James	25
John	15
Elmer	40

For one on one tutoring via skype at $35.00/Hr.; contact me at marksmathtutoring@yahoo.com

8.19) Given the graph below what is the mean, median, and mode

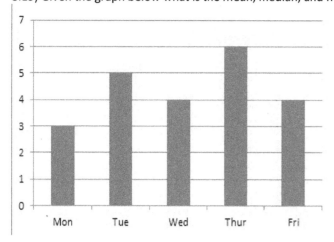

8.20) Given the graph below what is the mean, median, mode

8.21) Given the graph below what is the mean, median, mode

Croquis of a
Deliberate
Crime

YouTube

8.22) Given the graph below what is the mean, median, mode

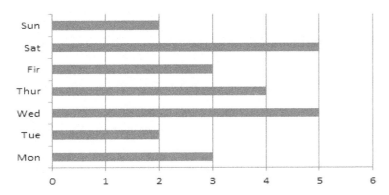

8.23) Given the graph below what is the mean, median, and mode of the dogs

8.24) Given the graph below what is the mean, median, and mode of mowing

Croquis of a
Deliberate
Crime

YouTube

9 ORDER OF OPERATIONS

9.1.1) 23x2+4   9.1.2) 16x3-6   9.1.3) 3x5x4   9.1.4) 3-6x7
9.1.5) 16+4÷2   9.1.6) 35÷7-2   9.1.7) 24x2-6   9.1.8) 13+6x2
9.1.9) 10÷4÷2   9.1.10) 12x3-6   9.1.11) 35-5÷5   9.1.12) 2+14÷7
9.1.13) 2-5x6   9.1.14) 3+4x3   9.1.15) 8÷2+6   9.1.16) 9÷3+3
9.1.17) 4+8÷4   9.1.18) 3x4÷2   9.1.19) 2x4x5   9.1.20) 21x3-6

9.1.21) 21+(4x6)   9.1.22) (2+3)x6   9.1.23) 5x(3+6)   9.1.24) 5÷(2+8)
9.1.25) (14x2)-6   9.1.26) (3+6)÷3   9.1.27) (12÷4)+4   9.1.28) (10x4)+6
9.1.29) 4+(2x4)   9.1.30) (3+6)x3   9.1.31) (10÷2)÷5   9.1.32) (12+3)÷5
9.1.33) (4x3)x2   9.1.34) (6÷2)÷3   9.1.35) (41-35)x2   9.1.36) (2x67)-4

9.1.37) 2(3)-3(1)   9.1.38) 3(4)+2(4)   9.1.39) 4(2)-3(5)   9.1.40) 5(2)-3(4)
9.1.41) 8(3)+3(5)   9.1.42) 2(7)-3(7)   9.1.43) 1(9)-0(6)   9.1.44) 2(5)+3(7)
9.1.45) 4(6)+5(2)   9.1.46) 5(1)-5(2)   9.1.47) 6(3)+2(4)   9.1.48) 5(2)-3(2)
9.1.49) 3x2+3x4   9.1.50) 6x2-4x5   9.1.51) 8÷2-6x3   9.1.52) 12÷3+3x4
9.1.53) 6x2+3x6   9.1.54) 2x5+4x7   9.1.55) 3x5-15÷3   9.1.56) 21÷3-4x2
9.1.57) 10x3-6x7   9.1.58) 35÷5+2x4   9.1.59) 12x3-2x6   9.1.60) 60÷6+2÷1

9.1.61)[2x(3+2)]-4   9.1.62) 4+[(5+2)x3] 9.1.63) 4-[(1x2)+3] 9.1.64) 15÷[(3x4)-7]
9.1.65) [3x(3+3)]+5 9.1.66) [3x(4+5)]-4 9.1.67) [(2+3)x2]÷5 9.1.68) [3x(7+3)]+3
9.1.69) [4x(3-2)]-11 9.1.70) 7÷[(2x3)+1] 9.1.71) [3x(3+6)]-5 9.1.72) [(4+4)x2]÷8
9.1.73) 10÷[(2x3)-1] 9.1.74) 2-[(3x2)+7] 9.1.75) 9-[(2x3)+3] 9.1.76) [2x(8+7)]-6
9.1.77) [10x(6+1)]-8 9.1.78) [3x(13+12)]-10 9.1.79) [2x(3-4)]-6 9.1.80) [(1+3)÷2]÷2

9.1.81) [2(4)-3(6)]+4   9.1.82) [4(1)+2(4)]-5   9.1.83) [4(1)-5(3)]+3   9.1.84) 3+[3(4)-2(6)]
9.1.85) [3(5)-2(8)]+10 9.1.86) [(4+1)x(2+3)]÷5 9.1.87) [(2+4)÷(2+1)]+3 9.1.88) [5(2)+3(4)]÷11
9.1.89) 5-[2(4)+3(5)]   9.1.90) [3(5)-4(4)]X5   9.1.91) 20÷[2(3)-1(1)] 9.1.92) 3X[2(3)-3(4)]
9.1.93) 5÷[5(4)÷2(2)]   9.1.94) 6X[4(5)-6(5)]   9.1.95) [2(3)+3(6)]+4   9.1.96) 10X2(3+5)

Croquis of a
Deliberate
Crime
YouTube

If you don't get the correct answer, and want an explanation on how to work the problem, go to YouTube and type in "MMT" then the problem number. An example would be, MMT 3.9.w12,. The video will show you how to work problem 3.9.w12.

For one on one tutoring via skype at $35.00/Hr.; contact me at marksmathtutoring@yahoo.com

100 ANSWER KEY

2.0 Definitions

2.1) B	2.2) D	2.3) C	2.4) C	2.5) B	2.6) D	2.7) 1
2.8) 7	2.9) D	2.10) D	2.11) B	2.12) A	2.13) C	2.14)C
2.15) B	2.16) B	2.17) A	2.18) B	2.19) A	2.20) A	2.21) A
2.22) 16, 94, 32		2.23) 37	2.24) 18	2.25) 20	2.26) 60	2.27) C
2.28) A	2.29) D	2.30) C	2.31) 227	2.32) 373.8	2.33) 748	2.34)A

3.1 Addition Single Digit

3.1.1) 4	3.1.2) 2	3.1.3) 10	3.1.4) 13	3.1.5) 5	3.1.6) 10
3.1.7) 3	3.1.8) 16	3.1.9) 9	3.1.10) 10	3.1.11) 11	3.1.12) 8
3.1.13) 9	3.1.14) 14	3.1.15) 7	3.1.16) 15	3.1.17) 6	3.1.18) 11
3.1.19) 4	3.1.20)12	3.1.21) 10	3.1.22) 14	3.1.23) 10	3.1.24) 13
3.1.25) 11	3.1.26) 15	3.1.27) 18	3.1.28) 9	3.1.29) 12	3.1.30) 9
3.1.31) 3	3.1.32) 15	3.1.33) 8	3.1.34) 7	3.1.35) 13	3.1.36) 6
3.1.37) 13	3.1.38) 16	3.1.39) 15	3.1.40) 7	3.1.41) 11	3.1.42) 11
3.1.43) 10	3.1.44) 13	3.1.45) 9	3.1.46) 14	3.1.47) 13	3.1.48) 12
3.1.49) 16	3.1.50) 9	3.1.51) 10	3.1.52) 14	3.1.53) 5	3.1.54) 11

3.2 Addition Two Digit

3.2.1) 34	3.2.2) 42	3.2.3) 50	3.2.4) 133	3.2.5) 105	3.2.6) 93
3.2.7) 56	3.2.8) 129	3.2.9) 70	3.2.10) 111	3.2.11) 59	3.2.12) 124
3.2.13) 107	3.2.14) 65	3.2.15) 136	3.2.16) 104	3.2.17) 72	3.2.18) 60
3.2.19) 74	3.2.20) 90	3.2.21) 151	3.2.22) 125	3.2.23) 88	3.2.24) 59
3.2.25) 108	3.2.26) 73	3.2.27) 85	3.2.28) 88	3.2.29) 87	3.2.30) 133
3.2.31) 83	3.2.32) 106	3.2.33) 105	3.2.34) 87	3.2.35) 111	3.2.36) 71
3.2.37) 55	3.2.38) 113	3.2.39) 121	3.2.40) 132	3.2.41) 164	3.2.42) 68
3.2.43) 121	3.2.44) 143	3.2.45) 120	3.2.46) 136	3.2.47) 55	3.2.48) 129

3.3 Addition Multiple Digit Addition

3.3.1) 2476	3.3.2) 2428	3.3.3) 503	3.3.4) 6990	3.3.5) 8323	3.3.6) 933
3.3.7) 1814	3.3.8) 1294	3.3.9) 6628	3.3.10) 1118	3.3.11) 600	3.3.12) 1253
3.3.13) 1081	3.3.14) 1065	3.3.15) 236	3.3.16) 1048	3.3.17) 732	3.3.18) 416
3.3.19) 974	3.3.20) 590	3.3.21) 651	3.3.22) 1025	3.3.23) 2288	3.3.24) 528
3.3.25) 531	3.3.26) 737	3.3.27) 861	3.3.28) 897	3.3.29) 878	3.3.30) 1333
3.3.31) 836	3.3.32) 1070	3.3.33) 1058	3.3.34) 5925	3.3.35) 11215	3.3.36) 589
3.3.37) 914	3.3.38) 3455	3.3.39) 1980	3.3.40) 1460	3.3.41) 3380	3.3.42) 276
3.3.43) 221	3.3.44) 643	3.3.45) 1120	3.3.46) 536		

3.12.1) 13.3	3.12.2) 2.22	3.12.3) 19.4	3.12.4) 13.3	3.12.5) 3.03
3.12.6) 63.3	3.12.7) 5.6	3.12.8) 8.58	3.12.9) 1.15	3.12.10) 77.7
3.12.11) 5.9	3.12.12) 39.85	3.12.13) 35.72	3.12.14) 6.5	
3.12.15) 9.64	3.12.16) 21.2	3.12.17) 4.68	3.12.18) 6	3.12.19) 13.465
3.12.20) 4.2327	3.12.21) 50.3	3.12.22) 84.75	3.12.23) 85.21	
3.12.24) 63.51	3.12.25) 5.675	3.12.26) 85.93	3.12.27) 75.73	
3.12.28) 38.342	3.12.29) 60	3.12.30) 1.253		

3.3.w1) 1078   3.3.w2) 749   3.3.w3) 197   3.3.w4) 499   3.3.w5) 82   3.3.w6) 17
3.3.w7) 129   3.3.w8) 305   3.3.w9) 157   3.3.w10) 784   3.3.w11) 627   3.3.w12) 22, 26
3.3.w13) 44   3.3.w14) A   3.3.w15) $690   3.3.w16) $44.05   3.3.17) 1195
3.3.w18) C   3.3.w19) A   3.3.w20) A   3.3.w21) D   3.3.w22) B   3.3.w23) B
3.3.w24) A   3.3.W25) D   3.3.w26) B   3.3.w27) D   3.3.w28) A   3.3.w29) 4:30
3.3.w30) 8:10   3.3.w31) 4:00   3.3.w32) 5:30

3.4 Subtraction Single Digits

3.4.1) 2 3.4.2) 2 3.4.3) 2 3.4.4) 1 3.4.5) 1 3.4.6) 4
3.4.7) 3 3.4.8) 3 3.4.9) 0 3.4.10) 13.4.11) 33.4.12) 1

3.4.55) -2   3.4.56) -8   3.4.57) -2   3.4.58) 13.4.59) 11   3.4.60) 1
3.4.61) 33.4.62) -2   3.4.63) -7   3.4.64) 03.4.65) 33.4.66) -4
3.4.67) -1   3.4.68) -4   3.4.69) -3   3.4.70) -3   3.4.71) 23.4.72) -5
3.4.73) 03.4.74) -4   3.4.75) 63.4.76) 43.4.77) 23.4.78) 3
3.4.79) -3   3.4.80) 13.4.81) 03.4.82) 93.4.83) 03.4.84) -5
3.4.85) -1   3.4.86) -1   3.4.87) 43.4.88) -1   3.4.89) 53.4.90) -4
3.4.91) 13.4.92) 03.4.93) 33.4.94) -5   3.4.95) 13.4.96) 7
3.4.97) -2   3.4.98) 53.4.99) -3   3.4.100) -4   3.4.101) 3   3.4.102) -2
3.4.103) 0   3.4.104) 5   3.4.105) 2   3.4.106) 0   3.4.107) 1   3.4.108) -7

3.5 Subtraction of Two Digits

3.5.1) 583.5.2) 2 3.5.3) 183.5.4) 373.5.5) 613.5.6) 13
3.5.7) 583.5.8) 333.5.9) 603.5.10) 13   3.5.11) 93.5.12) 46
3.5.13) 67   3.5.14) 73.5.15) 32   3.5.16) 90   3.5.17) 16   3.5.18) 56
3.5.19) 43.5.20) 32   3.5.21) 17   3.5.22) 71   3.5.23) 30   3.5.24) 39
3.5.25) 30   3.5.26) 51   3.5.27) 93.5.28) 74   3.5.29) 19   3.5.30) 25
3.5.31) 21   3.5.32) 93.5.33) 53   3.5.34) 25   3.5.35) 13.5.36) 9
3.5.37) 47   3.5.38) 51   3.5.39) 57   3.5.40) 18   3.5.41) 83.5.42) 44
3.5.43) 29   3.5.44) 61   3.5.45) 14   3.5.46) 62   3.5.47) 93.5.48) 29

3.5.49) -12   3.5.50) -8   3.5.51) 18   3.5.52) 17   3.5.53) -9   3.5.54) -27
3.5.55) -22   3.5.56) 33   3.5.57) -30   3.5.58) -37   3.5.59) -51   3.5.60) 46
3.5.61) 37   3.5.62) -33   3.5.63) -48   3.5.64) 80   3.5.65) 16   3.5.66) -4
3.5.67) -36   3.5.68) -18   3.5.69) 17   3.5.70) 71   3.5.71) -30   3.5.72) -21
3.5.73) -30   3.5.74) -51   3.5.75) 93.5.76) 64   3.5.77) -41   3.5.78) 25
3.5.79) -9   3.5.80) -70   3.5.81) 53   3.5.82) -25   3.5.83) -59   3.5.84) 9
3.5.85) -13   3.5.86) 13.5.87) 57   3.5.88) -2   3.5.89) -2   3.5.90) 34
3.5.91) 29   3.5.92) -9   3.5.93) -56   3.5.94) 62   3.5.95) -1   3.5.96) -67

3.6 Subtraction Multiple Digit

3.6.1) 746   3.6.2) 2026   3.6.3) 183   3.6.4) 140   3.6.5) 8279   3.6.6) 1029
3.6.7) 1736   3.6.8) 328   3.6.9) 6418   3.6.10) 234   3.6.11) 90   3.6.12) 755
3.6.13) 371   3.6.14) 67   3.6.15) 52   3.6.16) 792   3.6.17) 158   3.6.18) 272
3.6.19) 264   3.6.20) 82   3.6.21) 117   3.6.22) 71   3.6.23) 970   3.6.24) 110
3.6.25) 199   3.6.26) 483   3.6.27) 89   3.6.28) 639   3.6.29) 194   3.6.30) 247
3.6.31) 414   3.6.32) 594   3.6.33) 528   3.6.34) 4703   3.6.35) 1113   3.6.36) 53
3.6.37) 1038   3.6.38) 58   3.6.39) 138   3.6.40) 1034   3.6.41) 228   3.6.42) 2823
3.6.43) 1326   3.6.44) 102   3.6.45) 3132   3.6.46) 57   3.6.47) 214   3.6.48) 129
3.6.49) 191   3.6.50) 144   3.6.51) 2862   3.6.52) 38

3.6.53) -2254   3.6.54) -4974   3.6.55) -517   3.6.56) -6660
3.6.57) -1421   3.6.58) -271   3.6.59) -164   3.6.60) 328
3.6.61) 6418   3.6.62) -366   3.6.63) -910   3.6.64) -145
3.6.65) -129   3.6.66) -833   3.6.67) -148   3.6.68) -208
3.6.69) -2842   3.6.70) -7848   3.6.71) -736   3.6.72) -318
3.6.73) -83   3.6.74) -429   3.6.75) -2230   3.6.76) -290
3.6.77) 199   3.6.78) -517   3.6.79) 89   3.6.80) 639

3.13.1) 8.7   3.13.2) -1.78   3.13.3) -12.6   3.13.4) -0.3
3.13.5) -1.37   3.13.6) -56.7   3.13.7) -2.2   3.13.8) 7.62
3.13.9) 0.15   3.13.10) -70.3   3.13.11) 0.9   3.13.12) -38.15
3.13.13) -34.28   3.13.14) -3.3   3.13.15) -8.76   3.13.16) -2.8
3.13.17) 4.12   3.13.18) -0.4   3.13.19) 8.735   3.13.20) 0.2127
3.13.21) 18.3   3.13.22) -51.75   3.13.23) 80.81   3.13.24) -56.89
3.13.25) -2.125   3.13.26) 76.27   3.13.27) 54.73   3.13.28) 36.858
3.13.29) 9   3.13.30) 0.455

3.14.1) 25.3   3.14.2) 0.44   3.14.3) 54.4   3.14.4) 44.2   3.14.5) 1.826
3.14.6) 198   3.14.7) 6.63   3.14.8) 3.888   3.14.9) 0.325   3.14.10) 27.38
3.14.11) 8.5   3.14.12) 33.15   3.14.13) 25.2   3.14.14) 7.84
3.14.15) 4.048   3.14.16) 110.4   3.14.17) 1.232   3.14.18) 8.96
3.14.19) 26.2515   3.14.20) 4.47627   3.14.21) 548.8   3.14.22) 1126.125
3.14.23) 182.622   3.14.24) 199.262   3.14.25) 6.9225   3.14.26) 391.713
3.14.27) 684.915   3.14.28) 27.8992   3.14.29) 879.75   3.14.30) 0.340746

3.16.1) 1   3.16.2) -4   3.16.3) -2   3.16.4) 0
3.16.5) -6   3.16.6) -9   3.16.7) 2   3.16.8) -4
3.16.9) -11   3.16.10) 4   3.16.11) 5   3.16.12) -5
3.16.13) -10   3.16.14) -5   3.16.15) 5   3.16.16) 3
3.16.17) -2   3.16.18) 5   3.16.19) 1   3.16.20) -4
3.16.21) 13   3.16.22) 5   3.16.23) -10   3.16.24) 3
3.16.25) -4   3.16.26) -4   3.16.27) -7   3.16.28) -10
3.16.29) -1   3.16.30) -5

3.6.w1) A   3.6.w2) 99   3.6.w3) 29   3.6.w4) 44   3.6.w5) 1568   3.6.w6) A
3.6.w7) B   3.6.w8) 154   3.6.w9) A   3.6.w10) 474   3.6.w11) C   3.6.w12) 15
3.6.w13) 9353   3.6.w14) A   3.6.w15) 18850   3.6.w16) $4.50
3.6.w17) $10.76   3.6.w180 $7.88   3.6.w19) 88   3.6.w20) 7 Hrs. 25 Min
3.6.w21) 6 Hrs. 35 Min   3.6.w22) 6 Hrs. 20 Min   3.6.w23) 8 Hrs. 15 Min
3.6.w24) 261   3.6.w25) 47.47   3.6.w26) 14.72   3.6.w27) 9.76
3.6.w28) 60,345   3.6.w29) 13,320   3.6.w30) C   3.6.w31) 404
3.6.W32) 1.95   3.6.w33) 5:45   3.6.w34) 12:45   3.6.w35) 12:40
3.6.w36) 10:05   3.6.w37) 12:45   3.6.W38) B

3.7 Multiplication of Single Digits

3.7.1) 3 3.7.2) 0 3.7.3) 243.7.4) 403.7.5) 6 3.7.6) 21
3.7.7) 0 3.7.8) 633.7.9) 8 3.7.10) 25   3.7.11) 28   3.7.12) 12
3.7.13) 20   3.7.14) 45   3.7.15) 10   3.7.16) 54   3.7.17) 83.7.18) 24
3.7.19) 43.7.20) 32   3.7.21) 16   3.7.22) 45   3.7.23) 24   3.7.24) 40
3.7.25) 28   3.7.26) 56   3.7.27) 81   3.7.28) 03.7.29) 36   3.7.30) 14
3.7.31) 23.7.32) 56   3.7.33) 12   3.7.34) 12   3.7.35) 36   3.7.36) 5
3.7.37) 42   3.7.38) 64   3.7.39) 54   3.7.40) 6   3.7.41) 30   3.7.42) 18
3.7.43) 21   3.7.44) 36   3.7.45) 18   3.7.46) 45   3.7.47) 40   3.7.48) 35

3.7.49) 64   3.7.50) 14   3.7.51) 24   3.7.52) 49   3.7.53) 63.7.54) 18

3.8 Multiplication of Two Digit

3.8.1) 253	3.8.2) 440	3.8.3) 544	3.8.4) 4420	3.8.5) 1826	3.8.6) 1980
3.8.7) 663	3.8.8) 3888	3.8.9) 325	3.8.10) 2738	3.8.11) 850	3.8.12) 3315
3.8.13) 2520	3.8.14) 784	3.8.15) 4048	3.8.16) 1104	3.8.17) 1232	3.8.18) 896
3.8.19) 1045	3.8.20) 1944	3.8.21) 5628	3.8.22) 2646	3.8.23) 1711	3.8.24) 760
3.8.25) 2376	3.8.26) 682	3.8.27) 1786	3.8.28) 912	3.8.29) 1472	3.8.30) 4266
3.8.31) 1702	3.8.32) 1584	3.8.33) 2054	3.8.34) 1736	3.8.35) 2210	3.8.36) 1344
3.8.37) 714	3.8.38) 3192	3.8.39) 2848	3.8.40) 4355	3.8.41) 6723	3.8.42) 1431
3.8.43) 1395	3.8.44) 3450	3.8.45) 5092	3.8.46) 2812	3.8.47) 3663	3.8.48) 4368

3.9 Multiplication Multi Digit

3.9.1) 262,515   3.9.2) 447,627   3.9.3) 54,880   3.9.4) 1,126,125
3.9.5) 182,622   3.9.6) 199,262   3.9.7) 69,225   3.9.8) 391,713
3.9.9) 684,915   3.9.10) 278,992   3.9.11) 87,975   3.9.12) 340,746
3.9.13) 257,730   3.9.14) 110,084   3.9.15) 8448   3.9.16) 117,760
3.9.17) 127,715   3.9.18) 37,488   3.9.19) 101,745   3.9.20) 85,344
3.9.21) 104,228   3.9.22) 216,646   3.9.23) 65,511   3.9.24) 48,671
3.9.25) 60,590   3.9.26) 68,970   3.9.27) 183,350   3.9.28) 99,072
3.9.29) 151,512   3.9.30) 428,970   3.9.31) 172,875   3.9.32) 161,616
3.9.34) 210,145   3.9.35) 1,761,854 3.9.36) 22,779,864   3.9.37) 11,928
3.9.38) 195,853   3.9.39) 1,635,174 3.9.40) 540,531   3.9.41) 530,299
3.9.42) 403,744   3.9.43) 7595   3.9.44) 8050   3.9.45) 100,392
3.9.46) 130,416   3.9.47) 67,063

3.9.w1) 24	3.9.w2) 42	3.9.w3) 6	3.9.w4) 24	3.9.w5) 42	3.9.w6) C
3.9.w7) 72	3.9.w8) 7	3.9.w9) 63	3.9.w10) 4	3.9.w11) B	3.9.w12) C
3.9.w13) D	3.9.w14)584	3.9.w15) 36	3.9.w16) 768	3.9.w17)315	3.9.w18) B
3.9.w19) B	3.9.w20) B	3.9.w21) 72	3.9.w22) 18	3.9.w23) 35	3.9.w24) 48
3.9.w25) B	3.9.w26) B	3.9.w27) A	3.9.w28) C	3.9.w29) C	3.9.w30) 56
3.9.w31) C	3.9.w32) 384	3.9.w33) 592	3.9.w34) 6900	3.9.w35) 4032	3.9.w36) B

3.9.w37) 900   3.9.w38) 4800 3.9.w39) D 3.9.w40) $10,850   3.9.w41) B
3.9.w42) 1904   3.9.W43) $12,500   3.9.w44) 1176   3.9.w45) 48
3.9.w46) C   3.9.w47) C   3.9.w48) B   3.9.w49) D   3.9.50) 364
3.9.w51) 1264   3.9.w52) 125   3.9.w53) 837   3.9.w54) off season
3.9.w55) 18.75   3.9.w56) 10,272   3.9.w57) 4.81 lbs 3.9.w58) C
3.9.w59) 811   3.9.w60) 5 hrs. 15 min   3.9.w61) 3 hrs. 45 min
3.9.w62) 5:45   3.9.w63) 8 HRS. 2 min

3.10 Division

3.10.1) 23.10.2) 1   3.10.3) 33.10.4) 13.10.5) 43.10.6) 2
3.10.7) 13.10.8) 53.10.9) 13.10.10) 6   3.10.11) 3   3.10.12) 2

3.10.13) 1	3.10.14) 7	3.10.15) 1	3.10.16) 8	3.10.17) 4	3.10.18) 2
3.10.19) 1	3.10.20) 9	3.10.21) 3	3.10.22) 1	3.10.23) 10	3.10.24) 5
3.10.25) 2	3.10.26) 1	3.10.27) 12	3.10.28) 6	3.10.29) 4	3.10.30) 3
3.10.31) 2	3.10.32) 1	3.10.33) 14	3.10.34) 7	3.10.35) 2	3.10.36) 1
3.10.37) 15	3.10.38) 5	3.10.39) 3	3.10.40) 1	3.10.41) 6	3.10.42)3
3.10.43) 10	3.10.44) 3	3.10.45) 3	3.10.46) 3	3.10.47) 2	3.10.48) 5
3.10.49) 1	3.10.50) 4	3.10.51) 2	3.10.52)1	3.10.53) 4	3.10.54) 1

3.10.55) 34	3.10.56) 36	3.10.57) 32	3.10.58) 28
3.10.59) 56	3.10.60) 52	3.10.61) 61	3.10.62) 47
3.10.63) 53	3.10.64) 58	3.10.65) 26	3.10.66) 89
3.10.67) 83	3.10.68) 91	3.10.69) 43	3.10.70) 52
3.10.71) 81	3.10.72) 64	3.10.73) 64	3.10.74) 67
3.10.75) 68	3.10.76) 368	3.10.77) 216	3.10.78) 24
3.10.79) 28	3.10.80) 19	3.10.81) 26	3.10.82) 45
3.10.83) 45	3.10.84) 57	3.10.85) 46	3.10.86) 216
3.10.87) 16	3.10.88) 93	3.10.89) 74	3.10.90) 52
3.10.91) 149	3.10.92) 26	3.10.93) 56	3.10.94) 35
3.10.95) 94	3.10.96) 84	3.10.97) 1112	3.10.98) 35
3.10.99) 93	3.10.100) 35	3.10.101) 18	3.10.102) 34
3.10.103) 32	3.10.104) 21	3.10.105) 94	3.10.106) 76
3.10.108) 36	3.10.109) 287	3.10.110) 35	

3.10.113) 136	3.10.114) 64	3.10.115) 286	3.10.116) 127
3.10.117) 237	3.10.118) 17	3.10.119) 58	3.10.120) 194
3.10.121) 78	3.10.122) 61	3.10.123) 62	3.10.124) 47
3.10.125) 96	3.10.126) 283	3.10.127) 47	3.10.128) 36
3.10.129) 52	3.10.130) 85	3.10.131) 283	3.10.132) 47
3.10.133) 27	3.10.134) 99	3.10.135) 41	3.10.136) 148
3.10.137) 49	3.10.138) 32	3.10.139) 486	3.10.140) 194
3.10.141) 13	3.10.142) 84	3.10.143) 12	3.10.144)37

3.15.1) 4.8	3.15.2) 0.1	3.15.3) 0.2	3.15.4) 1.0
3.14.5) 0.4	3.15.6) 0.1	3.15.7) 0.4	3.15.8) 16.9
3.15.9) 1.3	3.15.10) 0.05	3.15.11) 1.36	3.15.12) 0.02
3.15.13) 0.02	3.15.14) 0.33	3.15.15) 0.05	3.15.16) 0.77
3.15.17) 15.71	3.15.18) 0.88		

3.17.1) -63	3.17.2) 27	3.17.3) -26	3.17.4) 36
3.17.5) -166	3.17.6) 180	3.17.7) 3.9	3.17.8) -32
3.17.9) -30	3.17.10) 21	3.17.11) -6	3.17.12) -255
3.17.13) -216	3.17.14) 4	3.17.15) -36	3.17.16) -9
3.17.17) 2	3.17.18) -2	3.17.19) -1	3.17.20) 3
3.17.21) -1	3.17.22) 2	3.17.23) -1	3.17.24) 3
3.17.25) -2	3.17.26) 9	3.17.27) -13	

3.10.w1) 4	3.10.w2)4	3.10.w3) 0	3.10.w4) 3	3.10.w5) 7	3.10.w6) 5
3.10.w7) A	3.10.w8) 7	3.10.w9) A	3.10.w10) B	3.10.w11) A	3.10.w12) B
3.10.w13) C	3.10.w14) B	3.10.w15) A	3.10.w16) 108	3.10.w17) 23	
3.10.w18) B	3.10.w19) B	3.10.w20) C	3.10.w21) B	3.10.w22) D	3.10.w23) D
3.10.w24) 27	3.10.w25) 24	3.10.w26) 180	3.10.w27) 34	3.10.w28) 170	
3.10.w29) 43	3.10.w30) B	3.10.w31) 57	3.10.w32) 60	3.10.w33) 21	3.10.w34) C
3.10.w35) D	3.10.w36) C	3.10.w37) A	3.10.w38) 6.35	3.10.w39) 37.5	
3.10.w40) 48	3.10.w41) C		3.10.W42) C	3.10.W43) 24	
3.10.w44) C	3.10.w45) 0.31	3.10.w46) 133		3.10.w47) 7.32 in	
3.10.w48) 33	3.10.w49) $137.51	3.10.w50) 127		3.10.w51) 55 min	
3.10.w52) 35 min	3.10.w53) 1 hr. 45 min	3.10.w54) 1 ht. 5 min			
3.10.w55) 6	3.10.w56) 6	3.10.w57) 7	3.10.w58) 7		

3.10.w59) 2   3.10.w60) 6   3.10.w61) 2   3.10.w62) 16

3.11 Inequalities

3.11.1) F   3.11.2) F 3.11.3) T 3.11.4) F 3.11.5) T 3.11.6) F

3.11.7) F 3.11.8) T 3.11.9) T 3.11.10) F   3.11.11) T   3.11.12) F

3.11.13) T	3.11.14) T	3.11.15) F	3.11.16) F	3.11.17) F	3.11.18) T
3.11.19) T	3.11.20) F	3.11.21) T	3.11.22) F	3.11.23) F	3.11.24) F

3.11.25) F	3.11.26) T	3.11.27) F	3.11.28) T		
3.11.29) F	3.11.30) T	3.11.31) F	3.11.32) F	3.11.33) F	3.11.34) F
3.11.35) F	3.11.36) F	3.11.37) F	3.11.38) F	3.11.39) F	3.11.40) T
3.11.41) T	3.11.42) T	3.11.43) F	3.11.44) F	3.11.45) T	3.11.46) F
3.11.47) F	3.11.48) F				

3.11.49) T	3.11.50) F	3.11.51) F	3.11.52) T	3.11.53) T	3.11.54) F
3.11.55) T	3.11.56) F	3.11.57) F	3.11.58) T	3.11.59) F	3.11.60) F
3.11.61) F	3.11.62) F	3.11.63) T	3.11.64) F	3.11.65) T	3.11.66) F
3.11.67) F	3.11.68) F	3.11.69) T	3.11.70) F	3.11.71) T	3.11.72) F

3.11.w1) A	3.11.w2) D	3.11.w3) D	3.11.w4) D	3.11.w5) C	3.11.w6) B
3.11.w7) C	3.11.w8) C	3.11.w9) C	3.11.w10) C		

4.1 Geometry

4.1) D	4.2) C	4.3) A, B, E, F, G		4.4) C	4.5) B
4.6) A	4.7) D	4.8) 9	4.9) 15	4.10) 18 4.11) 21	
4.12) B	4.13) A	4.14) 6	4.15) 120	4.16) 76 4.17) No	
4.18) C	4.19) A	4.20) YES	4.21) C	4.22) D	4.23) 4
4.24) 17 4.25) 22 4.26) 4		4.27) B	4.28) 28 4.29) 36M		
4.30) B	4.31) 153	4.32) 69 4.33) B		4.34) A	4.35) B
4.36) A	4.37) D	4.38) D	4.39) C	4.40) B	4.41) 8
4.42) 10 4.43) 125		4.44) 27 4.45) 72 4.46) 216		4.47) 24	
4.48) 64 4.49) 16 M^3		4.50) 240 ft^3	4.51) 64 ft^3	4.52) 125 m^3	4.53) 450
4.54) 225	4.55) 52 4.56) 156		4.57) B	4.58) A	4.59) C
4.60) C	4.61) D	4.62) D	4.63) A	4.64) B	4.65) D
4.66) C	4.67) C	4.68) A	4.69) A	4.70) D	4.71) C
4.72) A	4.73) B	4.74) B	4.75) C	4.76) 131	4.77) C
4.78) C	4.79) A	4.80) A	4.81) A	4.82) C	4.83) B
4.84) 260	4.85) 450	4.86) D			

5.0 Fractions

5.1   5.2)   5.3)   5.4)

For one on one tutoring via skype at $35.00/Hr.; contact me at marksmathtutoring@yahoo.com

5.5)   5.6)

5.7) Y   5.8) Y   5.9) N   5.10) Y   5.11) N
5.12) N   5.13) Y   5.14) N, 2/4<3/8 5.15) N, 2/3>3/6 5.16) N, 3/8<3/4
5.17) N, 1/3<3/8 5.18) N, 3/4>1/2 5.19) Y   5.20) y   5.21) N, 2/12<2/6
5.22) N, 2/6<2/3 5.23) y 2/4=4/8   5.24) N, 4/6>4/8   5.25) y, 6/12=3/6
5.26) Y, 3/4=9/12 5.27) N, 2/12<2/6   5.28) Y, 1/3=2/6   5.29) N, 1/8<1/4
5.30) B,3/4   5.31) C, 2/3   5.32) A 1/8   5.33) b, 8/12
5.34) A, 4/6   5.35) A, 7/8   5.36) Sarah, 1/3   5.37) 3/4 Lb.
5.38) You, 2/3 Lb. 5.39) Al, 3/4   5.40) 1/3   `5.41) 2/3
5.42) 3/5   5.43) 5/9   5.44) 3/5   5.45) 2/3
5.46) 3/8   5.47) 3/6   5.48) D, 7/8>5/8   5.49) D, 1/4<3/4
5.50) A, 5/6>4/6 5.51) D, 8/12>3/12   5.52) B, 3/8<6/8   5.53) A, 2/3>1/3
5.54) A   5.55) B   5.56) B   5.57) A
5.58) B   5.59) B   5.60) N   5.61) N
5.62) D   5.63) B   5.64) C   5.65) C
5.6.66) <   5.6.67) <

5.6.68) <   5.6.69) <   5.6.70) >   5.6.71) >5.6.72) <
5.6.73) >   5.6.74) >   5.6.75) <5.6.76) <5.6.77) <
5.6.78) <   5.6.79) <   5.6.80) >5.6.81) <5.6.82) >
5.6.83) <   5.6.84) <   5.6.85) <

Addition
5.2.1) 2/2   5.2.2) 5/3   5.2.3) 6/6   5.2.4) 5/4   5.2.5) 7/8   5.2.6) 10/9
5.2.7) 4/5   5.2.8) 6/6   5.2.9) 5/9   5.2.10) 6/7   5.2.11) 2/3   5.2.12) 5/6
5.2.13) 5/8   5.2.14) 5/7   5.2.15) 8/11   5.2.16) 9/16   5.2.17) 6/8   5.2.18) 5/7
5.2.19) 11/12   5.2.20) 12/13   5.2.21) 10/12   5.2.22) 12/15   5.2.23) 9/11   5.2.24) 11/10

5.2.25) 13/12   5.2.26) 15/18   5.2.27) 31/20   5.2.28) 11/14   5.2.29) 29/21   5.2.30) 20/21
5.2.31) 53/42   5.2.32) 11/10   5.2.33) 13/20   5.2.34) 73/56   5.2.35) 36/35   5.2.36) 15/28
5.2.37) 32/35   5.2.38) 11/24   5.2.39) 13/21   5.2.40) 26/48   5.2.41) 16/21   5.2.42) 23/21
5.2.43) 83/56   5.2.44) 45/28   5.2.45) 21/18   5.2.46) 5/6   5.2.47) 17/30   5.2.48) 38/24
5.2.49) 9/18   5.2.50) 10/24   5.2.51) 37/30   5.2.52) 43/25   5.2.53) 13/15   5.2.54) 17/12
5.2.55) 22/21   5.2.56) 70/48   5.2.57) 47/12   5.2.58) 118/24   5.2.59) 89/20   5.2.60) 302/56
5.2.61) 241/40   5.2.62) 233/42   5.2.63) 81/24   5.2.64) 159/40   5.2.65) 156/35   5.2.66) 31/12
5.2.67) 68/15   5.2.68) 202/35   5.2.69) 110/21   5.2.70) 235/56   5.2.71) 122/24   5.2.72) 87/12
5.2.73) 223/42   5.2.74) 145/24   5.2.75) 101/30   5.2.76)174/35   5.2.77) 77/30   5.2.78) 242/48
5.2.79) 211/40   5.2.80) 227/35   5.2.81) 110/21   5.2.82) 235/56   5.2.83) 156/32   5.2.84) 257/40
5.2.85) 101/20   5.2.86) 198/35   5.2.87) 213/56

5.2.88) 38/7   5.2.89) 61/8   5.2.90) 111/8   5.2.91) 67/6   5.2.92) 93/8   5.2.93) 125/9
5.2.94) 38/9   5.2.95) 66/7   5.2.96) 33/5   5.2.97) 60/7   5.2.98) 83/9   5.2.99) 78/9

5.2.100) 5/12   5.2.101) -11/15   5.2.102) -1/20   5.2.103) -4/32
5.2.104) -9/18   5.2.105) -26/21   5.2.106) -11/35   5.2.107) -13/20
5.2.108) -1/12   5.2.109) 2/24   5.2.110) 43/30   5.2.111) -2/12

5.2.112) -1/12   5.2.113) -22/15   5.2.114) -27/18   5.2.115) 23/15
5.2.116) -29/16   5.2.117) -47/12   5.2.118) -49/15   5.2.119) 7/12
5.2.120) -97/20   5.2.121) 22/16   5.2.122) -79/15   5.2.123) -6/8

5.2.124) 1/8   5.2.125) -13/3   5.2.126) -1/6   5.2.127) 1/5
5.2.128) -10/3   5.2.129) -21/4   5.2.130) -8/3   5.2.131) ¼

5.2.w1) 31/30   5.2.w2) 17/12   5.2.w3) 43/30
5.2.w4) 22/15   5.2.w5) 27/30   5.2.w6) 37/24
5.2.w7) 27/18   5.2.w8) 41/12   5.2.w9) 182/24
5.2.w10) 371/20   5.2.w11) 19/4

Subtraction

5.3.1) 0/2   5.3.2) 1/3   5.3.3) 4/6   5.3.4) 2/4   5.3.5) 2/8   5.3.6) 2/9
5.3.7) 1/5   5.3.8) 1/6   5.3.9) 1/9   3.3.10) 2/7   5.3.11) 0/3   5.3.12) 3/6
5.3.13) 1/8   5.3.14) 3/7   5.3.15) 1/11   5.3.16) 1/16   5.3.17) 8/8   5.3.18) 1/7
5.3.19) 1/12   5.3.20) 3/13   5.3.21) 1/12   5.3.22) 3/15   5.3.23) 3/11   5.3.24) 3/10

5.3.25) 5/12   5.3.26) 9/18   5.3.27) -1/20   5.3.28) -3/14   5.3.29) 1/21   5.3.30) 8/21
5.3.31) -17/42   5.3.32) 1/10   5.3.33) 3/20   5.3.34) -25/56   5.3.35) -6/35   5.3.36) 1/28
5.3.37) 18/35   5.3.38) -5/24   5.3.39) 1/72   5.3.40) -10/48   5.3.41) 2/21   5.3.42) -5/21
5.3.43) 13/56   5.3.44) 3/28   5.3.45) -9/18   5.3.46) -1/6   5.3.47) 7/30   5.3.48) -2/24
5.3.49) -3/18   5.3.50) 2/24   5.3.51) -13/30   5.3.52) 13/35   5.3.53) 7/15   5.3.54) 1/12
5.3.55) -8/21   5.3.56) -10/48   5.3.57) -7/12   5.3.58) -14/24   5.3.59) 39/20   5.3.60) 55/56
5.3.61) -31/40   5.3.62) -89/42   5.3.63) -17/14   5.3.64) -31/40   5.3.65) 44/35   5.3.66) -1/12
5.3.67) -28/15   5.3.68) -102/35   5.3.69) -44/21   5.3.70) -53/56
5.3.71) -14/24   5.3.72) -17/14   5.3.73) 41/42   5.3.74) -79/24
5.3.75) -31/30   5.3.76) -6/35   5.3.77) 7/30   5.3.78) 34/48
5.3.79) -99/40   5.3.80) -102/35   5.3.81) -34/21   5.3.82) -53/56
5.3.83) -3/8   5.3.84) -47/40   5.3.85) -11/40   5.3.86) -72/35
5.3.87) -59/56

5.3.100) 11/12   5.3.101) -1/15   5.3.102) 9/20   5.3.103) -12/32
5.3.104) -21/18   5.3.105) 2/21   5.3.106) 39/35   5.3.107) 3/10
5.3.108) -17/21   5.3.109) 34/24   5.3.110) 7/30   5.3.111) -10/12

5.3.112) 41/12   5.3.113) -22/15   5.3.114) -57/18   5.3.115) 77/15
5.3.116) 1/6   5.3.117) -31/12   5.3.118) -1/15   5.3.119) -49/12

5.3.120) 7/20   5.3.121) -68/16   5.3.122) -31/15   5.3.123) 46/8
5.3.124) 15/4   5.3.125) -5/3   5.3.126) -11/6   5.3.127) 19/5
5.3.128) -4/3   5.3.129) -5/4   5.3.130) -2/3   5.3.131) -15/4

5.3.w1) C   5.3.w2) 26 in   5.3.w4) A   5.3.w5) 1/20
5.3.w6) 1/10   5.3.w7) 1/36   5.3.w8) 7/18   5.3.w9) 13/45
5.3.w10) 37/35   5.3.w11) 41/20   5.3.w12) 57/20

Multiplication

5.4.1) 1/4   5.4.2) 2/9   5.4.3) 5/36   5.4.4) 3/16   5.4.5) 15/64   5.4.6) 24/81
5.4.7) 12/25   5.4.8) 20/36   5.4.9) 3/12   5.4.10) 2/12   5.4.11) 12/20   5.4.12) 2/14
5.4.13) 10/21   5.4.14) 4/21   5.4.15) 15/42   5.4.16) 3/10   5.4.17) 2/20   5.4.18) 21/56
5.4.19) 9/35   5.4.20) 2/14   5.4.21) 5/35   5.4.22) 1/24   5.4.23) 6/24   5.4.24) 3/48

5.4.25) 3/21   5.4.26) 6/21   5.4.27) 30/56   5.4.28) 18/28   5.4.29) 5/18   5.4.30) 1/6
5.4.31) 2/30   5.4.32) 15/24   5.4.33) 1/18   5.4.34) 1/24   5.4.35) 10/30   5.4.36) 12/35
5.4.37) 2/15   5.4.38) 6/12   5.4.39) 5/21   5.4.40) 25/48

5.4.41) 45/12   5.4.42) 195/24   5.4.43) 80/20   5.4.44) 135/56   5.4.45) 357/40   5.4.46) 84/24
5.4.47) 276/42   5.4.48) 112/14   5.4.49) 152/40   5.4.50) 160/35   5.4.51) 20/12   5.4.52) 64/15
5.4.53) 189/35   5.4.54) 121/21   5.4.55) 234/56   5.4.56) 153/24   5.4.57) 130/14   5.4.58) 286/42
5.4.59) 154/24   5.4.60) 77/30   5.4.61) 216/35   5.4.62) 49/30   5.4.63) 299/48   5.4.64) 217/40
5.4..65) 189/35   5.4.66) 121/21   5.4.67) 234/56   5.4.68) 189/32   5.4.69) 399/40   5.4.70) 126/20
5.4.71) 243/35   5.4.72) 187/56   5.4.73) 51`/7   5.4.74) 53/8   5.4.75) 355/8   5.4.76) 152/6
5.4.77) 189/8   5.4.78) 356/9   5.4.79) 33/9   5.4.80) 152/7   5.4.81) 52/5   5.4.82) 108/7
5.4.83) 74/9   5.4.84) 154/9

5.4.100) -2/12   5.4.101) 2/15   5.4.102) -1/28   5.4.103) -1/32
5.4.104) -5/18   5.4.105) 8/21   5.4.106) -10/35   5.4.107) 4/10
5.4.108) -6/12   5.4.109) -12/24   5.4.110) 15/30   5.4.111) -2/12

5.4.112) -35/12   5.4.113) 56/15   5.4.114) -35/18   5.4.115) -90/15
5.4.116) 35/6   5.4.117) 26/12   5.4.118) 40/15   5.4.119)-49/12
5.4.120) 117/20   5.4.121) -70/16   5.4.122) 88/15   5.4.123) -65/8

5.4.124) -14/4   5.4.125) 12/3   5.4.126) -5/6   5.4.127) -18/5
5.4.128) 7/3   5.4.129) 26/4   5.4.130) 5/3   5.4.131) -14/4

Division
5.5.1) 2/2   5.5.2) 6/3   5.5.3) 30/6   5.5.4) 12/4   5.5.5) 40/24
5.5.6) 54/36   5.5.7) 20/9   5.5.8) 30/24   5.5.9) 9/4   5.5.10) 12/3
5.5.11) 15/16   5.5.12) 4/7   5.5.13) 15/14   5.5.14) 14/6   5.5.15) 18/35
5.5.16) 6/5   5.5.17) 8/5   5.5.18) 24/49   5.5.19) 15/21   5.5.20) 8/7
5.5.21) 25/7   5.5.22) 3/8   5.5.23) 2/9   5.5.24) 8/18   5.5.25) 9/7
5.5.26) 9/14   5.5.27) 48/35   5.5.28) 24/21   5.5.29) 6/15   5.5.30) 2/3
5.5.31) 12/5   5.5.32) 18/20   5.5.33) 3/6   5.5.34) 6/4   5.5.35) 12/25
5.5.36) 15/28   5.5.37) 10/3   5.5.38) 9/8   5.5.39) 7/15   5.5.40) 30/40
5.5.41) 20/27   5.5.42) 52/90   5.5.43) 64/25   5.5.44) 119/64   5.5.45) 105/136
5.5.46) 63/32   5.5.47) 72/161   5.5.48) 32/49   5.5.49) 64/95   5.5.50) 56/100
5.5.51) 15/16   5.5.52) 20/48   5.5.53) 45/147   5.5.54) 33/77   5.5.55) 91/144
5.5.56) 54/68   5.5.57) 35/72   5.5.58) 132/91   5.5.59) 33/112   5.5.60) 35/66
5.5.61) 90/84   5.5.62) 42/35   5.5.63) 138/104   5.5.64) 56/155   5.5.65) 45/147
5.5.66) 33/77   5.5.67) 91/144   5.5.68) 72/84   5.5.69) 105/152
5.5.70) 45/56   5.5.71) 63/135   5.5.72) 77/136   5.5.73) 21/17
5.5.74) 8/53   5.5.75) 40/71   5.5.76) 48/19   5.5.77) 72/21
5.5.78) 89/36   5.5.79) 27/11   5.5.80) 38/28   5.5.81) 20/13
5.5.82) 18/42   5.5.83) 9/74   5.5.84) 22/63

5.5.100) -8/3   5.5.101) 6/5   5.5.102) -4/5   5.5.103) -4/8
5.5.104) -15/6   5.5.105) 12/14   5.5.106) -14/25   5.5.107) 5/8
5.5.108) -9/8   5.5.109) -18/16   5.5.110) 18/25   5.5.111) -6/4

5.5.112) -20/21   5.5.113) 42/20   5.5.114) -42/15   5.5.115) -50/27
5.5.116) 14/15   5.5.117) 39/8   5.5.118) 25/24   5.5.119) -21/28
5.5.120) 45/52   5.5.121) -28/40   5.5.122) 55/24   5.5.123) -20/26
5.5.124) -14/3   5.5.125) 9/4   5.5.126) -6/5   5.5.127) -10/9
5.5.128) 7/3   5.5.129) 26/4   5.5.130) 5/3   5.5.131) -14/4

5.5.132) $5^1/_2$ 5.5.133) $1^1/_3$ 5.5.134) $2^1/_4$ 5.5.135) 3

5.5.136) 5   5.5.137) $6^1/_2$ 5.5.138) 15   5.5.139) 3

5.5.140) $4^3/_7$ 5.5.141) 25   5.5.142) 7   5.5.143) 4

5.5.144) 7   5.5.145) $12^4/_6$ 5.5.146) $10^1/_4$ 5.5.147) $9^2/_7$

5.5.148) $11^1/_5$ 5.5.149) 19 ¾   5.5.150) $12^2/_8$ 5.5.151) $3^2/_5$

5.5.152) $21^2/_3$ 5.5.153) $21^2/_4$ 5.5.154) $42^1/_3$ 5.5.155) $11^1/_6$

5.5.156) $25^3/_5$ 5.5.157) $3^2/_4$ 5.5.158) 11   5.5.159) 55

5.5.160) 27   5.5.161) 18 ¼

5.5.162) 5   5.5.163) 4   5.5.164) 5   5.5.165) 1/3

5.5.166) 1/5   5.5.167) ½   5.5.168) 1/15   5.5.169) 1/3

5.5.170) 1/5   5.5.171) 1/15   5.5.172) 1/7   5.5.173) ¼

5,5,174) 1/7   5.5.175) 2/38   5.5.176) 1/11   5.5.177) 1/7

5.5.178) 25   5.5.179) 2/7   5.5.180) 3/2   5.5.181) 1/3

5.5.182) 2   5.5.183) 22   5.5.184) 1/42   5.5.185) 3/8

5.5.186) 16/3   5.5.187) 7/2   5.5.188) 11   5.5.189) 1/55

5.5.190) 1/27   5.5.191) 1/21

5.5.192) $4^2/_3$ 5.5.193) $13^1/_6$ 5.5.194) $3^1/_5$ 5.5.195) $6^1/_3$

5.5.196) 9 ½   5.5.197) 14 ¾   5.5.198) $25^1/_5$ 5.5.199) 21 ¾

5.5.200) $29^1/_3$ 5.5.201) $4^1/_5$ 5.5.202) $13^2/_3$ 5.5.203) $12^1/_5$

5.5.204) 6 ½   5.5.205) $8^1/_3$ 5.5.206) $9^2/_5$ 5.5.207) 11 ½

5.5.208) $38^1/_5$ 5.5.209) $15^1/_6$ 5.5.210) $9^2/_5$ 5.5.211) 28 ½

5.5.212) 25 ½   5.5.213) $12^5/_6$ 5.5.214) $20^1/_3$ 5.5.215) 19 ½

5.5.w1) 1/18   5.5.w2) 1/24   5.5.w3) 136   5.5.w4) 48/5 hrs

Inequalities

5.6.1) =   5.6.2) >   5.6.3) <   5.6.4) >   5.6.5) <   5.6.6) <

5.6.7) >   5.6.8) >   5.6.9) >   5.6.10) < 5.6.11) = 5.6.12) =

5.6.13) >   5.6.14) >   5.6.15) <   5.6.16) >   5.6.17) <   5.6.18) <

5.6.19) <   5.6.20) <   5.6.21) <   5.6.22) >   5.6.23) <   5.6.24) >

5.6.25) <   5.6.26) >   5.6.27) <   5.6.28) >   5.6.29) <   5.6.30) >

5.6.31) <   5.6.32) >   5.6.33) <   5.6.34) >   5.6.35) >   5.6.36) <

5.6.37) >   5.6.38) <   5.6.39) <   5.6.40) <   5.6.41) =   5.6.42) <

5.6.43) <   5.6.44) <   5.6.45) <   5.6.46) <   5.6.47) <   5.6.48) <

5.6.66) <   5.6.67) <   5.6.68) <   5.6.69) <   5.6.70) >   5.6.71) >

5.6.72) <   5.6.73) >   5.6.74) >   5.6.75) <   5.6.76) <   5.6.77) <

5.6.78) <   5.6.79) <   5.6.80) >   5.6.81) <   5.6.82) >   5.6.83) <

5.6.84) <   5.6.85) <

5.6.119) >   5.6.120) >   5.6121) <   5.6.122) <   5.6.123) >   5.6.124) >

5.6.125) <   5.6.126) >   5.6.127) >   5.6.128) <   5.6.129) <   5.6.130) >

5.6.131) >   5.6.132) <   5.6.133) <   5.6.134) <   5.6.135) >   5.6.136) <

5.6.137) >   5.6.138) >   5.6.139) <   5.6.140) <   5.6.141) >   5.6.142) <

5.6.143) <   5.6.144) >   5.6.145) <   5.6.146) <   5.6.147) >   5.6.148) >

5.6.149) <   5.6.150) <

5.6.251) <   5.6.252) <   5.6.253) >   5.6.254) >   5.6.255) <   5.6.256) >

5.6.257) <   5.6.258) <   5.6.259) <   5.6.260) <   5.6.261) <   5.6.262) <
5.6.263) <   5.6.264) <   5.6.265) <   5.6.266) <   5.6.267) <   5.6.268) >
5.6.269) <   5.6.270) <   5.6.271) <   5.6.272) >   5.6.273) >   5.6.274) <
5.6.275) <   5.6.276) <   5.6.277) <   5.6.278) <   5.6.279) <   5.6.280) <
5.6.281) <   5.6.282) <   5.6.283) >   5.6.284) <   5.6.285) <   5.6.286) >
5.6.287) >   5.6.288) >   5.6.289) >   5.6.290) >   5.6.291) >   5.6.292) <
5.6.293) <   5.6.294) <

5.6.w1) Mike   5.6.w2) C   5.6.w3) A   5.6.w4) C   5.6.w5) Guppy
5.6.w6) C   5.6.w7) C   5.6.w8) B   5.6.w9) B

5.7.1) $^{14}/_{10}$ or $1\,^{4}/_{10}$, 140% 5.7.2) $^{61}/_{10}$ or $6\,^{1}/_{10}$, 610% 5.7.3) $^{267}/_{100}$ or $2\,^{67}/_{100}$, 267%
5.7.4) $^{345}/_{100}$ or $3\,^{45}/_{100}$, 345%   5.7.5) $^{1878}/_{1000}$ or $1\,^{878}/_{1000}$, 187.8% 5.7.6) $^{935}/_{100}$ or $9\,^{35}/_{100}$, 935%
5.7.7) $^{14236}/_{100}$ or $142\,^{36}/_{100}$, 14236%   5.7.8) $^{225}/_{100}$ or $2\,^{25}/0_{10}$, 225%
5.7.9) $^{4325}/_{1000}$ or $4\,^{325}/_{1000}$, 432.5% 5.7.10) $^{1345/}_{100}$ or $13\,^{45}/_{100}$, 1345% 5.7.11) $^{71}/_{100}$ or 71%
5.7.12) $^{766}/_{100}$ or $7\,^{66}/_{100}$, 766%   5.7.13) $^{3578}/_{1000}$ or$3\,^{578}/_{1000}$, 357.8% 5.7.14) $^{55}/_{10000}$ or ,0.55%
5.7.15) $^{37}/_{100}$, 37%   5.7.16) $^{1235}/_{100}$ or $12\,^{35}/_{100}$,1235% 5.7.17) $^{32}/_{100}$, 32%
5.7.18) $^{16}/_{1000}$,, 1.6%   5.7.19) $^{113}/_{10}$ or $11\,^{3}/_{10}$, 113%   5.7.20) $^{1}/_{10}$, 1000%
5.7.21) $^{27676}/_{10000}$ or $2\,^{7676}/_{10000}$, 276.76%   5.7.22) $^{6257}/_{1000}$ or $6\,^{256}/_{1000}$, 625.7%
5.7.23) $^{1735}/_{100}$ or $17\,^{35}/_{100}$, 1735% 5.7.24) $^{125}/_{1000}$, 12.5%   5.7.25) $^{91}/_{10}$ or $9\,^{1}/_{10}$, 910%
5.7.26) $^{346}/_{100}$ or $3\,^{46}/_{100}$,346%   5.7.27) $^{399}/_{100}$ or $3\,^{99}/_{1000}$, 399%   5.7.28) $^{101}/_{100}$ or $1\,^{1}/_{100}$, 101%
5.7.29) $^{341}/_{100}$ or $3\,^{41}/_{100}$, 341%   5.7.30) $^{125}/_{1000}$, 12.5%

5.8.1) 0.04, 4%   5.8.2) 0.27, 27%   5.8.3) 0.013, 1.3%   5.8.4) 0.3, 30%
5.8.5) 0.67, 67%   5.8.6) 0.012, 1.2%   5.8.7) 1.27, 127% 5.8.8) 0.03, 3%
5.8.9) 0.034, 3.4%   5.8.10) 1.7, 170% 5.8.11) 3.04, 304%   5.8.12) 1.002, 100.2%
5.8.13) 0.6,60%   5.8.14) 2.3, 230% 5.8.15) 3.5, 350% 5.8.16) 0.04, 4%
5.8.17) 4.01, 401%   5.8.18) 2.047, 204.7%   5.8.19) 2.137, 213.7%   5.8.20) 3.4, 340%
5.8.21) 16.7, 1670%   5.8.22) 3.003, 300.3%   5.8.23) 0.89, 89% 5.8.24) 1.27, 127%
5.8.25) 0.14, 14% 5.8.26) 0.006, 0.6%   5.8.27) 0.29, 29% 5.8.28) 0.009, 0.9%
5.8.29) 16.23, 1623%   5.8.30) 1.045, 104.5%

5.8.31) 0.7, 76%   5.8.32) 0.7, 67%   5.8.33) 0.7, 67%   5.8.34) 0.5, 50%
5.8.35) 1.1, 114% 5.8.36) 2.3, 233% 5.8.37) 0.8, 75%   5.8.38) 0.2, 20%
5.8.39) 0.3, 29% 5. 8.40) 1.3, 133%   5.8.41) 0.2, 17%   5.8.42) 0.8, 80%
5.8.43) 0.6, 57%   5.8.44) 0.3, 33%   5.8.45) 0.2, 22%   5.8.46) 1, 100%
5.8.47) 1.3, 133% 5.8.48) 0.3, 33%   5.8.49) 1.4, 140% 5.8.50) 1.7, 167%
5.8.51) 0.5, 50%   5.8.52) 0.4, 40%   5.8.53) 1, 100%   5.8.54) 2.5, 250%
5.8.55) 1.5, 150% 5.8.56) 1.5, 150% 5.8.57) 0.4, 43%   5.8.58) 0.3, 33%
5.8.59) 1.2, 120% 5.8.60) 0.6, 60%

5.8.61) 36/100, 0.36   5.8.62) $1^{28}/_{100}$, 1.28   5.8.63) 2/100, 0.02,   5.8.64) 65/100,0.65
5.8.65) 0.12, 12/100   5.8.66) 39/100, 0.39   5.8.67) $1^{61}/_{100}$, 1.16   5.8.68) 23/100, 0.23
5.8.69) 51/100, 0.51   5.8.70) $1\,^{46}/_{100}$, 1.46   5.8.71) $4\,^{36}/_{100}$, 4.36   5.8.72) $2\,^{25}/_{100}$, 2.25
5.8.73) 87/100, 0.87   5.8.74) $1\,^{77}/_{100}$, 1.77   5.8.75) $2\,^{18}/_{100}$, 2.18   5.8.76) 4/100, 0.04
5.8.77) $1\,^{69}/_{100}$, 1.69   5.8.78) 47/100, 0.47   5.8.79) $3\,^{1}/_{100}$, 3.01   5.8.80) $2\,^{59}/_{100}$, 2.59
5.8.81) $3\,^{26}/_{100}$, 3.26   5.8.82) $2\,^{69}/_{100}$, 2.69   5.8.83) $2\,^{51}/_{100}$, 2.51   5.8.84) 78/100, 0.78

5.8.w1) C

5.10.w1) B	5.10.w2) B	5.10.w3) D	5.10.w4) C	5.10.w5) C	5.10.w6) C
5.10.w7) A	5.10.w8) A	5.10.w9) A	5.10.w10) A	5.10.w11) B	5.10.w12) C
5.10.w13) B	5.10.w14) D	5.10.w15) B	5.10.w16) B	5.10.w17) A	5.10.w18) D
5.10.w19) B	5.10.w20) B,C	5.10.w21) B	5.10.w22) B	5.10.w23) B	5.10.w24) C
5.10.w25) A					

6.0 GRAPHING

6.1) 4	6.2) 350	6.3)B	6.4)D	6.5) A	6.6) 500LBS
6.7) B	6.8) 20 MIN	6.9) A	6.10) C	6.11) D	6.12) B
6.13) C	6.14) C	6.15) A	6.16) C	6.17) D	6.18) C
6.19) B	6.20) 5	6.21) 5	6.22) 10 6.23) 55 6.24) 10		
6.25) C	6.26) B	6.27) 1	6.28) 44 6.29) A	6.30) D	
6.31) B	6.32) C	6.33) C	6.34) (5,5)	6.35) A	6.36) (2,2)
6.37) C	6.38) C	6.39) D	6.40) B	6.41) D	6.42) B
6.43) 3	6.44) C				

7.0 MEASURING

7.1) 3 CM   7.2) 6IN 7.3) A=1IN, B=2IN, C=$2\frac{1}{2}$IN, D=$\frac{1}{2}$ IN   7.4) 18

7.5) ½ IN	7.6) 3:00	7.7) D	7.8) D	7.9) B	7.10) 30
7.11) D	7.12) C	7.13) B	7.14) 96 7.15) 175	7.16) 17	
7.17) 340	7.18) C	7.19) C	7.20) C	7.21) C	7.22) D
7.23) A	7.24) B	7.25) C 7.26) D	7.27) C	7.28) A	
7.29) A	7.30) C	7.31) C	7.32) C	7.33) A	7.34) B
7.35) A	7.36) A	7.37) A	7.38) D	7.39) C	7.40) C
7.41) D	7.42) C	7.43) D	7.45) 1 in	7.46) 92.5	7.47) 77.5
7.48) 1	7.49) 1 ½	7.50) 3 ½	7.51) 4:35	7.52) 7:10	7.53) 4:25
7.54) 4:30	7.55) 6:25	7.56) 10:05			

8.0 STATISTICS

8.1)A	8.2) A	8.3) Sugar and Mint	8.4) B	8.5) 10/30 or 1/3
8.6) 2/7 8.7) 6/12 or 1/2	8.8) 49/105	8.9) 1/24	8.10) 112/157	
8.11) 6/14	8.12) 12/12	8.13) 1/3	8.14) 5/7	

8.15) Mean = 56, median = 60, mode = 60

8.16) Mean = 88.25, Median = 80, Mode = no mode

8.17) Mean = 48.75, Median = 52.5, Mode = no mode

8.18) Mean = 28.75, Median = 30, Mode = no mode

8.19) Mean = 4.4, Median = 4, Mode = 4

8.20) Mean =16, Median = 15, Mode = 15

8.21) Mean = 6, Median = 6, Mode = no mode

8.22) Mean = 7.29, Median = 3, Mode = 2, 3, 5

8.23) Mean = 41.25, Median = 42.5, Mode = no mode

8.24) Mean = 46.25, Median = 47.5, Mode = no mode

For one on one tutoring via skype at $35.00/Hr.; contact me at marksmathtutoring@yahoo.com

9.0 Order of Operations

9.1.1) 509.1.2) 429.1.3) 609.1.4) -39   9.1.5) 329.1.6) 3
9.1.7) 429.1.8) 259.1.9) 5 9.1.10) 30   9.1.11) 69.1.12) 4
9.1.13) -28   9.1.14) 15   9.1.15) 10   9.1.16) 69.1.17) 69.1.18) 6
9.1.19) 40   9.1.20) 57

9.1.21) 45   9.1.22) 30   9.1.23) 45   9.1.24) 5/10 or ½
9.1.25) 22   9.1.26) 39.1.27) 79.1.28) 46   9.1.29) 12   9.1.30) 27
9.1.31) 19.1.32) 39.1.33) 24   9.1.34) 19.1.35) 12   9.1.36) 130

9.1.37) 39.1.38) 20   9.1.39) -7   9.1.40) -2   9.1.41) 99.1.42) -7
9.1.43) 99.1.44) 31   9.1.45) 34   9.1.46) -5   9.1.47) 26   9.1.48) 4
9.1.49) 18   9.1.50) -8   9.1.51) -14   9.1.52) 16   9.1.53) 30   9.1.54) 38
9.1.55) 10   9.1.56) -1   9.1.57) -12   9.1.58) 15   9.1.59) 24   9.1.60) 12

9.1.61) 69.1.62) 25   9.1.63) -1   9.1.64) 39.1.65) 23   9.1.66) 23
9.1.67) 29.1.68) 33   9.1.69) -7   9.1.70) 19.1.71) 22   9.1.72) 2
9.1.73) 29.1.74) -11   9.1.75) 09.1.76) 24   9.1.77) 62   9.1.78) 65
9.1.79) -8   9.1.80) 1

9.1.81) 14   9.1.82) 79.1.83) -8   9.1.84) 3
9.1.85) 99.1.86) 59.1.87) 59.1.88) 29.1.89) -18   9.1.90) -5
9.1.91) 49.1.92) -18   9.1.93) 19.1.94) -60   9.1.95) 28   9.1.96) 160

Croquis of a
Deliberate
Crime

YouTube

If you don't get the correct answer, and want an explanation on how to work the problem, go to YouTube and type in "MMT" then the problem number. An example would be, MMT 3.9.w12,. The video will show you how to work problem 3.9.w12.

For one on one tutoring via skype at $35.00/Hr.; contact me at marksmathtutoring@yahoo.com

CPSIA information can be obtained
at www.ICGtesting.com
Printed in the USA
LVHW062345220123
737736LV00012B/644